THE
AUSTIN
PROTOCOL
COMPILER

Advances in Information Security

Sushil Jajodia
Consulting editor
Center for Secure Information Systems
George Mason University
Fairfax, VA 22030-4444
email: jajodia@gmu.edu

The goals of Kluwer International Series on ADVANCES IN INFORMATION SECURITY are, one, to establish the state of the art of, and set the course for future research in information security and, two, to serve as a central reference source for advanced and timely topics in information security research and development. The scope of this series includes all aspects of computer and network security and related areas such as fault tolerance and software assurance.

ADVANCES IN INFORMATION SECURITY aims to publish thorough and cohesive overviews of specific topics in information security, as well as works that are larger in scope or that contain more detailed background information than can be accommodated in shorter survey articles. The series also serves as a forum for topics that may not have reached a level of maturity to warrant a comprehensive textbook treatment.

Researchers as well as developers are encouraged to contact Professor Sushil Jajodia with ideas for books under this series.

Additional titles in the series:

Additional information about this series can be obtained from
http://www.wkap.nl/prod/s/ADIS

THE
AUSTIN
PROTOCOL
COMPILER

by

Tommy M. McGuire
Mohamed G. Gouda
The University of Texas at Austin

Springer

eBook ISBN: 0-387-23228-1

ISBN: 978-1-4419-3588-5   eBook ISBN: 978- 0-387-23228-7

Visit Springer's eBookstore at: http://ebooks.springerlink.com
and the Springer Global Website Online at: http://www.springeronline.com

To Dianne Driskell.
                    T.M.M.

*To the memory of my
parents.*
                    M.G.G.

This page intentionally left blank

CONTENTS

This page intentionally left blank

PREFACE

There are two groups of researchers who are interested in designing network protocols and who cannot (yet) effectively communicate with one another concerning these protocols. The first is the group of protocol verifiers, and the second is the group of protocol implementors.

The main reason for the lack of effective communication between these two groups is that these groups use languages with quite different semantics to specify network protocols. On one hand, the protocol verifiers use specification languages whose semantics are abstract, coarse-grained, and with large atomicity. Clearly, protocol specifications that are developed based on such semantics are easier to prove correct. On the other hand, the protocol implementors use specification languages whose semantics are concrete, fine-grained, and with small atomicity. Protocol specifications that are developed based on such semantics are easier to implement using system programming languages such as C, C++, and Java.

To help in closing this communication gap between the group of protocol verifiers and the group of protocol implementors, we present in this monograph a protocol specification language called the Timed Abstract Protocol (or TAP, for short) notation. This notation is greatly influenced by the Abstract Protocol Notation in the textbook *Elements of Network Protocol Design,* written by the second author, Mohamed G. Gouda. The TAP notation has two types of semantics: an abstract semantics that appeals to the protocol verifiers and a concrete semantics that appeals to the protocol implementors group.

More significantly, we show in this monograph that the two types of semantics of TAP are equivalent. Thus, the correctness of a TAP specification of some protocol, that is established based on the abstract semantics of TAP, is maintained when this specification is implemented based on the concrete semantics of TAP. The equivalence between the abstract and concrete semantics of TAP suggests the following three-step method for developing a correct implementation of a protocol:

1. Specify the protocol using the TAP notation.

2. Verify the correctness of the specification based on the abstract semantics of TAP.

3. Implement the specification based on the concrete semantics of TAP.

To aid in step 3 of this method, we developed the Austin Protocol Compiler (or APC, for short) that takes as input a TAP specification of some protocol and produces as output C-code that implements this protocol based on the concrete semantics of TAP. The design of the Austin Protocol Compiler is one of the main features of this monograph.

This monograph is primarily directed towards protocol designers, verifiers, reviewers, and implementors. It is also directed towards graduate students who are interested in designing, verifying, and implementing network protocols.

The authors wish to express their thanks to their friends and colleagues at the Department of Computer Sciences at The University of Texas at Austin for their encouragement and support.

The Austin Protocol Compiler software, including the compiler, runtime system, and the examples from this book, is available from the Austin Protocol Compiler home page[1].

---

[1]http://www.cs.utexas.edu/users/mcguire/software/apc/

ACKNOWLEDGEMENTS

The authors would like to thank Lorenzo Alvisi, Michael D. Dahlin, Mootaz Elnozahy, and Aloysius K. Mok for their suggestions which have improved this monograph.

Tommy M. McGuire would like to thank his friends and coworkers in UTCS and elsewhere for their support: Kay Nettle, Fletcher Mattox, John Chambers, Stephanie Tomlinson, Dan Machold, Cyndy Matuszek, Toren Smith, Joe Trent, Scott Sutcliffe, Chris McCraw, Tony Bumpass, Casey Cooper, Pat Horne, Chris Kotrla, Matt Larson, Bart Phillips, Carol Hyink, Lewis Phillips and his ex-boss, Patti Spencer. Without their patience, this work would not have been completed. He is also grateful for the support and encouragement of his family.

Mohamed G. Gouda is grateful to his parents from whom he inherited his moral pursuit and work ethics. His mother, an art teacher and a school principal in Cairo, was born on June 29, 1917 and passed away on September 10, 2002. His father, a language teacher and an education official in Cairo, was born on April 1, 1916 and passed away on June 3, 1996. This monograph is dedicated to their living and loving memory.

T.M.M.
M.G.G.
Austin, TX
July, 2004

This page intentionally left blank

Chapter 1

NETWORK PROTOCOLS

A network protocol is the set of rules necessary to allow two or more computational processes to communicate with each other. These processes may be executing on the same machine or on different machines connected by many different kinds of networks. The processes may be separate operating system processes, running different programs; or may be virtual processes, modular parts of a single program; or may be components of the operating system. The key factors are that there are more than one process and that they must communicate with each other.

As computational processes, the processes communicate by exchanging well-defined messages across a communication channel, and the nature of this exchange defines the rules making up a network protocol. The most conspicuous part of these rules is the format of the messages which the processes exchange. More importantly, however, the rules describe the computation that each of the processes must make in order to send the correct message containing the correct values at the correct time.

The rules making up the network protocol, both the message formats and the computations, are embodied by programs, and the development of both the abstract rules and the concrete programs is the subject of this work.

Protocol development problems

Network protocol development presents a number of problems beyond those of developing traditional serial programs. Many of these problems are shared with other parallel and distributed programming tasks, but many more are unique to network protocols. The problems fall into one of three classes:

1. Intrinsic problems.

2. Extrinsic problems.

3. Compatibility problems.

Intrinsic problems. In general, the intrinsic problems in network protocol development include the same classes of safety and liveness problems associated with any distributed or parallel program. In any communicating system, whether it is a parallel or distributed program or a network protocol, the ordering of events is not well determined: many events may happen at once and a given sequence of events may not be repeatable. The number of potential orderings seriously hinders development, particularly when it is based on intuitions gained from serial programs.

Beyond those classes of problems, intrinsic problems in network protocol development include two two further areas: communication errors and security problems.

Communication errors such as message loss or message corruption are not normally seen in general distributed or parallel programming. (Although a distributed program may be running in an environment subject to such errors, it is usually built on a network protocol that hides the errors.) However, these errors are very common in the environment of message-passing network protocols; common enough to need to be a basic feature of the conceptual model for network protocols.

Security problems should be considered an intrinsic problem of network protocols, although they are often not. Some aspects of security in a network protocol are confidentiality; integrity; authorization; authentication and its converse, anonymity; and non-repudiation and its converse, plausible deniability. All of these aspects should be treated as intrinsic problems for a protocol since the number of possible attacks on each aspect make it impossible to foresee all of them—conceptually, correcting vulnerabilities is easier than defending against attacks.

Intrinsic problems of a network protocol apply, and can be described, in isolation, without reference to any systems outside the processes and channels involved in the protocol. For that same reason, they can also be handled in isolation. Common, successful techniques for handling intrinsic problems use formal methods such as correctness verification and model checking.

Extrinsic problems.   While many of the intrinsic problems of network protocol development are shared with the development of any distributed or parallel
program, other issues are unique to network protocols. The environment of
the network protocol introduces extrinsic problems of network protocol development, and unfortunately, these extrinsic problems are often not solvable by
the same methods as the intrinsic problems. There are certainly interactions
between some extrinsic problems and the intrinsic problems described previously. For example, while communication errors themselves are best considered intrinsic faults, many characteristics of their occurrence are not. Consider
a protocol which sends a large number of small messages back-to-back, with
no delay between messages, across a network containing a router which, when
congested, drops the most recently received messages. The protocol may be
expecting uncorrelated message loss errors, allowing at least some messages
through the network, but in this case message losses are not uncorrelated—the
router will tend to drop the entire burst or at least the trailing portion of the
burst. In this case, the behavior of the protocol may be intrinsically correct, but
unsatisfactory in use.

On the other hand, extrinsic problems also include non-error issues such as
the effects of the protocol on other instances of the protocol or other protocols
sharing the same network. These issues are significantly different from intrinsic problems. A protocol's correct behavior may cause congestion collapse in
a network shared by many instances of the protocol, or may starve other protocols of network resources that must be shared. In general, such behavior cannot
be seen by examining the protocol in isolation; it often only becomes visible
with experience running a new protocol.

One set of examples of extrinsic problems in protocol development lies
in the original HyperText Transport Protocol, both versions 0.9 and (according to the default behavior) 1.0[1]. The fundamental idea behind HTTP was
originally quite simple—the client opens a Transmission Control Protocol, or
TCP, connection with the server, makes a request, and reads the response. The
closing of the connection by the server indicates the end of the response; from
the client's viewpoint, the connection resembles a normal file I/O stream. Two
problems with this simple approach are:

1. Opening a TCP connection requires a three-message handshake and closing the connection may require four messages[2, 3].[1] Since the request
   and response are normally fairly small, the connection management messages represented a significant part of the traffic involved in the request.
   Since much of the cost of the work in the network is effectively per-
   message, this inefficiency primarily impacted the network itself.

2. Between the round trips of the connection establishment and TCP's
   congestion avoiding slow-start behavior, the connection-per-request approach resulted in significant latency[4, 3]. One response to this latency
   was to use multiple connections to the same server to make several related requests simultaneously. Since congestion-control information was
   not shared between connections, this response makes the overall set of
   requests (for the resources associated with a single web page, for example) behave in a more aggressive fashion in terms of congestion control,
   again impacting the network[5].

The newer version of HTTP, 1.1 [6], attempts to solve those two problems by
keeping connections alive for multiple requests and by multiplexing several
requests simultaneously on the same connection. As a result, HTTP 1.1 is no
longer simple.

Compatibility problems. The final class of problems in network protocol
development does not directly concern the protocol itself, but rather the network protocol development process, including interoperability, extensions, and
enhancements. Generally, all of the components of a distributed or parallel
program are developed together, as part of the same effort. Different protocol
components, such as different processes communicating by using a protocol or
different implementations of the same process in a given protocol, are not—
a process on one machine may communicate with a process on a completely
different type of machine elsewhere, with both processes being developed independently in space and time. If protocol development does not center around a
coherent specification of the protocol, interoperability between the components
suffers.

---

[1]It is possible to piggy-back the connection closing flags on data messages, but many traces
of TCP connections do not show such behavior.

A related problem involves changes in the protocol itself. After using a network protocol for a period of time, additional features may need to be added to the protocol or existing behavior of the protocol may need to be changed. Since parts of the protocol are implemented separately, the altered protocol should be capable of continuing to interoperate with the previous version. While the details of such changes are not foreseeable, if the original development of the protocol does not include the possibility, the protocol may later need to be scrapped entirely or its existence and inflexibility may hinder future progress.

Existing solutions

There are many successful methods of handling each of these problems, although not all methods cover all of the problems successfully.

The most visibly successful method is used by the Internet Engineering Task Force and the Internet community. This method is based on natural-language protocol standards documents, the Internet Drafts and the Request For Comments series, along with interoperating implementations. The process for Internet standards, including protocols, is described in RFC2026[7]. The goals of the process, from RFC2026, are:

> In general, an Internet Standard is a specification that is stable and well-understood, is technically competent, has multiple, independent, and interoperable implementations with substantial operational experience, enjoys significant public support, and is recognizably useful in some or all parts of the Internet.

Unfortunately, standards documents are frequently large and imprecise. Often the only formal specifications of a protocol are the implementations, which are often not identified in the standards, are frequently not available for inspection, and are themselves far from concise or understandable. For instance, Wright and Stevens in Volume 2 of *TCP/IP Illustrated*[8] present much of the code from the BSD4.4 TCP/IP suite implementation, and it is a rather large volume. Additionally, as can be seen from *TCP/IP Illustrated,* the implementation often hides the important details of a protocol in a larger mass of code; important details handling intrinsic or extrinsic issues frequently comprise only a small fraction of the implementation, while these details require a great deal of research and constitute the largest part of the difficulties in protocol development. For example, Nagle's algorithm[9], which adaptively inhibits small messages in TCP connections and thus helps avoid network congestion collapse, requires approximately four lines of code in *TCP/IP Illustrated*'s presentation. Refinements to Nagle's algorithm, originally published in 1984, are still being suggested; for example, by Minshall, *et al.,* in 1999[10].

The key to understanding and implementing any complex system with vital but minuscule details, particularly in such an ad-hoc environment, is modularization. In the case of network protocols, modularization almost always involves layering.

Protocol layering

Modularization proceeds by identifying some aspect of a system and encapsulating that aspect as a component behind some interface which allows other components to manipulate it while hiding the details of the component. In network protocols, each component is a layer, conceptually built using the services provided by a lower layer and in turn providing services to a higher layer.

Figure 1 shows the most common illustration of such layering, the International Standards Organization's (ISO) Open Systems Interconnect (OSI) reference model[11]. In this model, each layer communicates with the layers above and below it, and conceptually, with the corresponding layer in some other process. In practice, this model provides notation and descriptive terms; it is not commonly used for implementations.

Figure 1.2 shows a similar model used by the Internet protocols. It has been referred to as the hourglass model, since the Internet Protocol acts as a common unifying layer. In contrast with the OSI model, this model is the basis for the implementation of the Internet, not only from the standpoint of the operating system's code, but also in the layout of the messages exchanged—as each message is sent, each descending layer prepends any information it uses to the message as a header and as each message is received, each ascending layer removes the corresponding header.

For support in developing layered protocols, one framework, the x-Kernel[12, 13], stands out. The x-Kernel provides an efficient scaffolding for

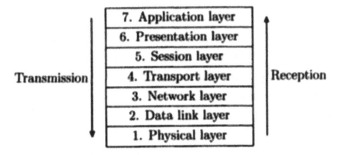

Figure 1.1: The OSI Reference Model. Messages being sent logically descend through the layers; messages being received ascend.

Application layer (SMTP, NNTP, HTTP, etc.)
Transport layer (TCP, UDP, SCTP, RTP, etc.)
Internet layer (IP)
Network layer (Ethernet, ATM, etc.)

Figure 1.2: The Internet model (the hourglass).

assembling a number of network protocol layers, where each layer is implemented independently using the library provided by the x-Kernel.

Unfortunately, layering introduces a new sin: the layering violation. Like the crime of heresy, a layering violation may only be visible within its own model. Specifically, a layering violation occurs when a layer n inappropriately uses an interface of a layer greater than $n + 1$ or less than $n - 1$.

While such violations often indicate a failure in the modularity of the design, in many cases layering becomes a goal itself[2], resulting in contorted protocol designs. For example, one feature of TCP that has caused layering violation arguments is Path MTU discovery[14]. The maximum transmission unit (MTU) of a network link is the maximum size message that can be sent over the link. The Path MTU (PMTU) is the smallest of the MTUs in the network between two processes. If a process sends a message that is larger than the MTU for a link, IP will fragment the message into parts small enough to pass

---

[2] In fact, Peterson and Davie[13] define *protocol* in terms of the layers.

through the link. These fragments are not reassembled until all reach the destination process and the loss of a single fragment results in the loss of the whole message. Fragmenting and reassembling messages also requires processing time from network components which may not have it to spare—routers, in the first case, and the critical path for incoming messages, in the second. For these and other reasons, protocols such as TCP would prefer not to have their messages fragmented. On the other hand, these protocols would also prefer to use the largest message possible, since that reduces the overhead needed for the communication.

The potential layering violation revolves around the fact that MTU sizes are attributes of network layers below IP, while the protocols attempting to identify the best message size are above IP and IP does not provide them with path MTU information. Path MTU discovery uses the "don't fragment" flag in IP messages, which causes an IP router to drop any message that is too large and respond with an ICMP "can't fragment" error message. TCP (or another higher-layer protocol) can receive this error and then adjust its transmissions to find the largest workable message size. Whether this is a layering violation or not, RFC1191, describing path MTU discovery, is a Draft Standard on the Internet Architecture Board Standards Track.

There are similar arguments around explicit congestion notification[15] and many other useful techniques. The proliferation of these and other techniques leads to the IETF being described as a "architectural pretzel factory"[16]. In response, Braden, Farber, and Handley[17] propose a "role-based architecture" as an non-layered alternative; whether it will be successful as such is an open question.

The problems with HTTP described previously also demonstrate the difficulties with a layered architecture—these problems show a conflict between the behavior of HTTP and the intended use of TCP. Unfortunately, since the development of congestion-controlled transport protocols such as TCP and the deployment of such protocols are both difficult, adding another transport protocol with semantics better matched to HTTP's behavior did not occur.

Protocol frameworks

In Figure 1.2, the distance in terms of behavior between what the protocols of the transport layer provide and what the protocols of the application layer need is broad. Since many similar application protocols make individual choices from a relatively limited set of behaviors, protocol frameworks can be designed to bridge this distance, in effect supplying intermediary layers specifically designed for a class of applications.

Birman, *et al.* [18, 19], have developed several such frameworks (such as Horus and Ensemble) based on micro-protocols and layering, where protocol components implementing various behaviors can be assembled (somewhat like Lego blocks) to create a system combining the behaviors. Unfortunately, the protocol composition style does not necessarily take into account inter-micro-protocol behavioral relationships which do not allow arbitrary composition.[3]

Another framework is the Blocks Extensible Exchange Protocol, BEEP[20, 21]. The BEEP framework is designed to handle asynchronous, message-passing, connection-oriented application protocols, and to provide for the following aspects of application behavior[22]:

- framing, which tells how the beginning and ending of each message is delimited;

- encoding, which tells how a message is represented when exchanged;

- reporting, which tells how errors are described;

- asynchrony, which tells how independent exchanges are handled;

- authentication, which tells how the peers at each end of the connection are identified and verified; and,

- privacy, which tells how the exchanges are protected against third-party interception or modification.

These aspects are described by "profiles" which define the syntax and semantics of the messages exchanged. BEEP offers a great deal of flexibility for

---

[3] Specifically, in one presentation, two blocks labelled "compression" and "encryption" were shown composed both ways; unfortunately, these two components cannot be arbitrarily composed because encryption results in incompressible data.

handling much of the complexity in designing application protocols. Unfortunately, the framework needed to provide the flexibility is quite complicated: For example, Rose[21] says, "Messages are arbitrary MIME [Multipurpose Internet Mail Extensions] content, but are usually textual (structured using XML [the eXtensible Markup Language])".

Although these frameworks are quite successful in their intended environment, their size and complexity limit their applicability in environments with restricted space or computational power, in addition to the limits imposed by their area of focus. Also, they are built with, and intended to be used with, code written in a traditional programming language. As described previously, most programming languages obscure the network protocol-specific issues and problems.

Finally, while frameworks provide flexibility, this flexibility is only available in the domain of the framework—using a framework outside its design domain is likely to be an uphill battle.

Protocol languages

Frameworks, such as those described previously, serve primarily as runtime support for code written in a traditional programming language. Like the ad hoc techniques described earlier, they have two limitations:

- Traditional programming languages do not highlight network protocol-specific behavior, and impede understanding the protocol's intrinsic, extrinsic, and compatibility issues.

- The frameworks' size and complexity appear at runtime. (Although some frameworks such as Ensemble minimize their runtime footprint by performing optimizations at compile-time, such efforts are limited by the granularity of the framework.)

An alternative approach is to create a notation intended for network protocols, in order to deal with one or both of those limitations. Most research in this area is aimed at the first limitation, as it is the most difficult.

Notations or domain specific languages intended for network protocols come in two varieties: permissive and strict.

Permissive notations.   Permissive notations are designed primarily to make implementation easy. These notations expose the behavior of the protocol, and are often very flexible, but are not typically intended to address protocol development problems formally and verifiably.

A fine example of a permissive notation is Prolac[23, 24], a statically-typed, object-oriented programming language designed for network protocols. The explicit goals of Prolac are readability, efficiency, evolvability, and behavioral predictiblity. This predictability, however, does not come based on formal reasoning, but rather on informal specifications and easing their translation into code. Also, Prolac omits any protocol-specific abstractions such as message transmission. As a result, Prolac lacks a strong semantic grounding for verification. Approaches with similar, but less extreme, limitations are taken in Morpheus[25] and Promela++[26].

On the other hand, Teapot[27], a language for writing cache coherence protocols, is primarily a permissive notation, generating C code, but is also capable of generating a model specification for the **MurΦ** model checker[28]. The combination, as described by Chandra[29], highlights the power of a domain-specific language linked with formal methods.

Likewise, ESP[30, 31, 32] is a language for describing event-driven state machines for programmable devices with limited CPU and memory resources. The ESP compiler generates both efficient C code and Promela models for checking the the state machines. However, ESP is not designed for network protocols, and is not intended for human verification.

Strict notations.   Strict notations are aimed primarily at making correctness verification easy and only secondarily (if at all) at implementation. The primary distinction among the strict notations is whether they are intended for automatic model checking or manual verification. The notations intended for automatic model checking often have a more complex, flexible structure, but oppose that flexibility with tight limits necessary for efficient model checking, such as a requirement that the models have a finite state. Notations intended for manual verification have a much simpler structure, because the complexity of the notation seriously impairs human verification, but do not place arbitrary limits on the protocol under study.

Two strict, very abstract notations are Unity[33] and TLA+[34]. Unfortunately, as Chandy and Misra say when comparing Unity with other programming approaches, "[The] generality of Unity is also its limitation when applied to a specific class of problems." Other strict notations more focused on communications are Estelle, LOTOS, and SDL[35], the UDP Calculus[36], and Promela[37, 38, 39]. These notations differ in a number of areas, including their complexity and ability to express network protocols specifically, but all are grounded in high-level abstraction. The tools available for each lean towards verification and model checking aids rather than executable interpreters or compilers. Indeed, due to the complexity and abstraction, protocols compiled from these notations, if such is possible at all, frequently exhibit poor performance. Finally, the compilers required are themselves complex programs.

On the other end of the strict notations is Esterel[40]. Esterel is a synchronous language intended for specifying protocol behavior abstractly, but Castelluccia, *et al.* [41], describe a compiler for protocols that generates efficient code. On the other hand, Esterel is not focused on message-passing network protocols and it is neither sufficiently abstract to easily verify protocols nor sufficiently simple to easily implement them.

The Austin Protocol Compiler

The Austin Protocol Compiler, and the Timed Abstract Protocol notation, are the subject of this work. The Timed Abstract Protocol notation, or TAP, is a small, simple language designed specifically for describing asynchronous message-passing network protocols with the ultimate goal of verification. TAP is based on the Abstract Protocol notation, or AP, developed by Gouda[42], which takes a very abstract, high level approach to network protocols. Unfortunately, like several of the other strict notations described previously, AP makes very strong guarantees about time, concurrency, and failure that make protocol verification easy but protocol implementation difficult.

For example, in AP a timeout is an action guarded by a global predicate: the decision whether the action may be executed can potentially be based on the values of variables in remote processes and the contents of the network between processes as well as the local state. Also, AP guarantees that actions, made up of an arbitrary sequence of statements, and errors, which come from a small class, must execute atomically and fairly, and that messages are propagated through the channels of the network immediately.

The guarantees of AP make it impractical to implement directly. Further, expressing some of the major sources of complexity in some protocols is difficult, since AP does not provide a direct model of time. TCP[43, 44] itself is one example that exposes this problem. This protocol is founded on a sliding-window protocol for transferring data, but the majority of the complexity in TCP involves *when* messages are to be sent—the round-trip time, from the sender to the receiver and back, and the retransmission time for lost messages are important factors to TCP. These factors are precisely those which are difficult to express in the high-level of abstraction of AP.

Therefore, the Timed Abstract Protocol notation modifies AP slightly, preserving the ease of verification while adding the ability to express temporal behavior and moving slightly towards implementability. It also has *two* execution models: a high-level, abstract model allowing protocols to be understood and verified readily, and a low-level, concrete model which makes efficient implementation possible. The relationship between these two models, which is described in detail later, is complex. However, in short, for many protocols the two models are equivalent—a protocol implemented according to the concrete model behaves the same as a protocol understandable in the abstract model.

The final piece of the protocol development puzzle is the Austin Protocol Compiler, or APC, which can transform a process described in TAP into executable code in C. The combination of the Timed Abstract Protocol notation with the Austin Protocol Compiler satisfies the original three classes of network protocol development problems in the following ways:

1. The simple domain-specific language of TAP, with its underlying formal model, addresses the intrinsic problems of protocol development through its clarity and verifiability.

2. The clarity of the TAP language, along with the fast turn-around of a compiler, allows practical experience with a protocol while it is still in development.

3. The formal TAP notation, with its emphasis on the protocol's details, and the ability of the compiler to create a running reference model create an environment where the compatibility problems in protocol development can be handled.

The next chapter discusses the TAP notation in detail, and the following chapter presents the two execution models. Subsequently, Chapter 4 and Chapter 5 argue the equivalence of the two execution models. Then, Chapter 6 describes the Austin Protocol Compiler and its runtime system. The following two chapters present examples of the use of the TAP notation and APC. A final chapter contains concluding remarks.

Chapter 2

THE TIMED ABSTRACT PROTOCOL NOTATION

The Timed Abstract Protocol notation, or TAP, is designed to be a small language for describing asynchronous, message passing network protocols. This focus entails several features:

- TAP is intended to describe protocols which normally wait for an externally generated event such as a received message or a timeout, then perform local computation to handle the event. As a result, the processes in TAP are made up of guarded actions, where the guards are based on the availability of a received message, or a timeout occurance as well as local state.

- Network protocols generally deal with two kinds of information: *protocol control information,* which is mainly made up of integral values and process addresses, and *data,* which is uninterpreted by the protocol. Also, the processing of a protocol at a local level is usually simple and should terminate quickly. Following these two observations, the state of processes is limited to minimal control information and the control structures are kept simple. These limitations serve to ease understanding and verification.

- Specialized operations, such as sending a message, are necessary for asynchronous message passing protocols. These operations are integrated into the language where they have specific semantics, again easing understanding and verification.

In TAP, a network protocol consists of two or more processes, which communicate by sending messages across channels. In this chapter, we begin to present the syntax and general semantics of TAP by discussing a simple example protocol.

Messages and channels

In TAP, a message is a sequence of fields, where each field is either an integral value consisting of protocol control information or a byte array containing un-interpreted data. The integral fields can be either constant or variable; constant fields can be used to distinguish messages while variable fields carry protocol information. For example, Figure 2.1 shows two messages, each of which has a single, constant field identifying it. Figure 2.1 does not show the full range of options; variable fields would not specify values and data fields would specify the field size in bytes, with either a constant or non-constant expression.

```
message rqst                          message rply
begin                                 begin
    type : 8 bits = 0                     type : 8 bits = 1
end                                   end
```

Figure 2.1: Request/reply messages.

A channel is a queue of messages. Messages are inserted into the tail of the queue by the sending process and removed from the head by the receiving process.

When discussing a protocol, the contents of a channel are referred to by a sequence of messages surrounded by angle brackets and separated by semi-colons: $<m;n>$. A channel itself is referred to by the notation **ch.**p.q, where p and q are the names of the sending process and the receiving process, respectively.

In the TAP notation, channels are implicit—they are identified by the abstract addresses of the sending and receiving processes. Since each process is itself one of the endpoints, only the remote address is needed within a process; the name of the process identifies the address of its local endpoint.

Every process is connected to every other process by channels in both directions. As a result, every process can send messages to any other process it has the address of.

Processes

A process consists of a local state and a set of actions describing the behavior of the process. Figure 2.2 shows the two processes of a simple request/reply protocol.

```
process p                      process q
const q : address              var p : address
var readyp : boolean = true    begin
begin                            rcv rqst from p  →
    readyp  → send rqst to q;        send rply to p
                readyp := false  end
  | rcv rply from q  →
        readyp := true
end
```

Figure 2.2: Request/reply protocol, version 1.

The local state of a process is described by variables and constants, of one of a number of data types. There are two data types used in processes p and q in Figure 2.2:

1. An **address** is used to identify a channel between the current process and another, either to send a message to another process or to recognize the sender of a received message.[1]

2. A **boolean** is either true or false.

The remaining basic data type, **integer,** has values from 0 to $2^{32} - 1$. The syntax of TAP also allows smaller ranges of integers as well as multidimensional arrays of any of these data types.

---

[1]An address is special in that it cannot be assigned a literal value in TAP. Instead, its value must be provided by the environment of the process. As described later, variable addresses receive values when used in receive guards. Additionally, the Austin Protocol Compiler runtime system provides the capability to set addresses outside the executable code generated by the compiler.

Actions

Actions describe the computation performed by a process. Each action consists of a guard, describing the circumstances under which the action is enabled, and a body, providing the statements which are executed when the action is executed.

When discussing protocol computations, the individual actions are referred to by the notation $p.n$, where p is the name of the process and n is the number of the action within the process. Similarly, $p.id$ refers to a variable or constant id in a process p.

There are two kinds of action guards in Figure 2.2:

1. A local guard is a Boolean predicate involving the local state of the process. The action is enabled when the predicate is true. An example of a local guard is that of p.1, the first action of process p in Figure 2.2. The guard of this action is the predicate readyp.

2. A receive guard identifies a message and the address of a remote process and is enabled when a matching message is at the head of the channel from a remote process. An example is p.2, the second action of process p. The guard of this action is **rcv** rply **from** q, which is enabled when a rply message is at the head of the channel form q to p. When this action is selected for execution, as discussed later, the rply message will be removed from the channel.

   Again, the address here is special—a receive guard with a constant address will only be enabled when the matching message is at the head of the channel from the process identified by the address. On the other hand, a receive guard with a variable address is enabled when the matching message is at the head of the channel from *any* process; during the execution of the action, the address variable takes as its value the address of the remote process.

Statements

Most of the statements in TAP are relatively conventional. There are two kinds of statements in Figure 2.2:

- The first is a send statement, **send** rqst **to** q. This statement inserts the message rqst into ch.p.q.

- The second is an assignment statement, such as readyp := **false.** TAP supports multiple assignment, where a list of variables on the left-hand-side is matched by a list of expressions on the right-hand-side.

When a message is received or sent by an action, it introduces a message structure that is local to the action. This message structure has records labeled by the field names from the message. When a message is received, the records contain the values of the fields from the incoming message. The values of the fields of messages to be sent can be set by assigning to the records before sending the message. These structures, however, do not participate in the state of the process because they are not preserved between actions.

The statements are sequentially combined by separating them with a semicolon.

Additional statements are also available in TAP:

- The **skip** statement does nothing.

- A conditional statement,

$$\textbf{if } p_0 \rightarrow s_0 \parallel p_1 \rightarrow s_1 \parallel \ldots \parallel p_n \rightarrow s_n \textbf{ fi,}$$

 chooses a branch $p_i \rightarrow s_i$ nondeterministically from the branches with true predicates among $p_0, \ldots p_n$ and executes the corresponding statement s_i.

- The iteration statement, **do** $p \rightarrow s$ **od,** executes statement s repeatedly, as long as predicate p is true.

Protocol style

A number of issues apply to the design of protocols specified in the TAP notation. One is illustrated in Figure 2.2: protocol quiesence. Another two are loop termination, and conditional completeness.

The protocol should be quiescent: it should not be possible for any process in the protocol to continue executing local actions indefinitely. An action, in

TAP, is executed *when* its guard is enabled; this is at variance with AP, where an action is executed *only when* its guard is enabled. The difference is that a process in TAP cannot wait when an action is enabled. For example, if an action sending a message has a **true** local guard, the action will flood the network with instances of mesasge it sends.

Instead, every process in the protocol should only execute a finite number of local actions before every local action becomes disabled—this prevents the process from abusing local resources. Such a process can instead wait for a message to be received or for a timeout to expire.

A related issue is loop termination. Although neither process p nor process q needs a **do** statement, other protocols will, and the necessity that actions be atomic requires that loops terminate deterministically, and preferably after performing only the computations needed by the protocol. This prevents the execution of a single action from blocking all of the other computations of a process.

Finally, the conditional statement syntactically uses multiple branches, each with a boolean predicate and a body of statements. For clarity, the predicates should be mutually exclusive, so that a single branch is possible in any state, and the disjunction of the predicates should be true, so that some branch is taken from any state.

Justification

The TAP notation is intended to specify message-passing network protocols simply and clearly. Each of the features of the notation supports this goal:

1. The message specification describes the minimal features needed for most common messages of existing protocols. It is neither as complete nor as complex as other message specification languages such as ASN.1[45] and XDR[46]. Instead, the TAP message notation is restricted to describing a simple format which is interoperable with many Internet protocols while allowing the programmer the flexibility to deal with other messages.

2. Processes have a simple structure, particularly in the definition of their local state and the limited set of actions used to describe their behavior.

Coupled with the execution model, described in the next chapter, these features make reasoning about network protocols easier.

3. Like Promela[39], Teapot[27], Esterel[40], and other formal notations, TAP tries to avoid fine-grained data manipulation while expressing overall control structure. The statements describing the behavior of actions are limited in number and simplified, when compared with general purpose languages. This simplification, first, eases reasoning about the behavior, and second, reduces the tendency to include overly complex behavior or behavior unrelated to the network protocol in the specification.

This chapter has only described the basic syntax and semantics of TAP. The details of TAP computations are the subject of the next chapter. However, the next section contains a detailed discussion of the TAP language, based on its grammar. Understanding the next section is not necessary in order to understand subsequent chapters.

Details of TAP

In previous sections, we examined the TAP notation from an abstract viewpoint, as a formal notation for specifying network protocols. Much of the remainder of this work will continue with that viewpoint, but this section examines the TAP notation as a programming language.

The discussion of the complete of the TAP language follows the structure of the TAP grammar—it re-covers the parts of TAP described previously and includes features of TAP that will not be described fully until the next chapter as well as features that are not further mentioned. The grammar is described using the Extended Backus-Naur Format, with the following conventions:

- {...} indicates zero or more copies of the contained elements.

- [...] indicates zero or one copy of the contained elements; i.e. the contents are optional.

- (...|...) indicates a choice between the contained elements.

- Literal text is presented in quotation marks.

- Non-literal token elements are in italics. There are three of these:

  - A *string* is a quote-delimited string of characters which does not span lines. Internal quotes and newlines can be escaped by a back-slash. These strings cannot be manipulated in TAP, but can serve as arguments to functions as well as to directives as described later.

  - A *number* is one or more decimal digits, indicating a non-negative number.

  - An *id* is an identifier, made up of a letter followed by any number of letters or numbers.

Parsing of each source file begins with the start symbol:

> start ::= elements
> elements ::= {element}
> element ::= **"import"** *string*
> | **"include"** *string*
> | message
> | process

The source file given to the compiler consists of a sequence of elements. Each element is either an import directive, an include directive, a message definition, or a process definition.

The import directive looks for the file named in the *string*. The contents of this file are read and processed by the compiler before any subsequent elements in the current source file.

The include directive inserts a C include directive in the output file, calling for the file named by the *string*. These included files form part of the interface between the APC-generated C module and external C code.

Message syntax

> message ::= m-header m-body
> m-header ::= ["**external**"] "**message**" m-name [m-functs]
> m-name ::= *id*
> m-functs ::= "(" m-in "," m-out ")"
> m-in ::= *id*

m-out ::= *id*
m-body ::= **"begin"** fields **"end"**
fields ::= {field **","**} field

Each message definition consists of a header and a body. The message header primarily provides a name for the message. The body of the message is a sequence of fields, separated by commas. The message definition is used by the compiler to produce:

1. A C structure with records for each field in the message.

2. Parsing and marshalling functions, which interpret and recognize received messages and convert a message structure to a sequence of bytes for transmission, respectively.

Optionally, the message can be marked as external, in which case the compiler does not generate the C functions for marshalling and parsing the message. This allows the programmer to provide such functions, in order to handle more complex messages than those that can be described by TAP. Also optionally, two functions can be identified which process the message immediately after the fields in the message have been parsed (m-in) and immediately before the message is sent (m-out). These functions receive the message buffer as well as the structure describing the fields of the message, allowing them to compute a checksum for the message, for example.

field ::= f-name **":"** f-type [**"="** f-value]
f-name ::= *id*
f-value ::= expression

Each field definition consists of a field-name, a field-type, and optionally, a field-value. If the field-value is present, the field is considered constant; the field is automatically set to that value before the message is sent and received messages are checked to ensure the field contains the proper value as part of the process of recognizing messages. In these expressions, the only allowable values are constants and the names of previous fields.

f-type ::= f-size (**"bits"** | **"bytes"**)
f-size ::= expression

A field-type describes the size and type of the contents of the field. The expression describing the size can contain literal values or the names of previous fields in the message. The type of the field is implied by the use of bits or bytes to describe the field.[2]

- A bit field contains an unsigned integer value. The size expression describes the size of the field in bits; it must not be larger than 32 bits.

- A byte field contains a sequence of data bytes. The size expression describes the size of the field in 8-bit bytes. For a received message, the value of the record for the field in the structure generated by the compiler will be a pointer to the data in the original message buffer. When building a message to be sent, the value of the record should be set to a pointer to a sequence of bytes which will remain valid until the message is sent.

Each message has an additional field, named size, which indicates the overall size of the message in bytes. When receiving a message terminating with an arbitrary-length data field, the size field (minus the size of any previous fields) provides the length of the final field. When sending such a message, assigning to the size field allows the message marshalling functions to copy the appropriate number of bytes from the array pointed to by the data field.

Process syntax

> process ::= p-header p-body
> p-header ::= **"process"** p-name [constants] [variables]
> p-name ::= *id*
> constants ::= **"const"** declarations
> variables ::= **"var"** declarations
> declarations ::= {declaration **";"**} declaration
> p-body ::= **"begin"** actions **"end"**

Each process definition also consists of a header and a body. The process header provides a name for the process as well as the optional declarations for

---

[2] For grammatical correctness, **"bit"** is allowed as a synonym for **"bits"** and likewise, **"byte"** for **"bytes"**.

the process's constants and variables. The process's body contains a sequence of actions.

> declaration ::= ids ":" type ["=" initial-value]
> ids ::= {*id* ","} *id*
> type ::= "**integer**"
> | *number* ".." *number*
> | "**boolean**"
> | "**address**"
> | "**array**" "[" array-size "]" "**of**" type
> array-size ::= *number*
> initial-value ::= (*number* | "**true**" | "**false**")

In each declaration, a sequence of identifiers which name constants or variables are associated with a type and optionally an initial value. The basic types allowed by TAP are 32-bit integers, booleans, and addresses. The integer type can be specified as either a general integer or as a range of allowed values.

The initial values for variables or constants must match the type of the variable or constant; the value of an integer is a number, and the value of a boolean is either true or false. Addresses may not be given an initial value in TAP. (The initial value of an address can be given via the C interface while initializing the APC runtime system. See Chapter 6 for more information.)

The only complex type supported by TAP is the array, with any number of dimensions. The allowed indices of each array dimension is given by the array-size value; indices range from 0 to the array-size–1. If an initial value is given for an array, each element of the array is set to the value.

Action syntax

> actions ::= {action "[]"} action
> action ::= guard "->" statements
> guard ::= (local-guard | receive-guard | timeout-guard)
> local-guard ::= expression
> receive-guard ::= "**rcv**" m-name "**from**" address
> address ::= *id*
> timeout-guard ::= "**timeout**" t-name

t-name ::= *id*

In a TAP process, actions are separated by a box, written as two square brackets: [ ]. Each action consists of a guard and a sequence of statements. There are three forms of guards: local, receive, and timeout. Chapter 3 describes the behavior of each of the guards in more detail, and Chapter 6 contains the details of the runtime support for each guard.

Local guards are made up of a predicate, a boolean expression. The action is enabled when the guard evaluates to true.

Receive guards specify a message accepted by the action and an address. The guard may be enabled if and only if the received message matches the message specified by the receive guard. If the address is a constant, then the action will only be enabled if the message is from the process identified by the address. If the address is a variable, then the action will be enabled no matter where the message is from and the address will be set to the source of the message.

Timeout actions provide a name, t-name, for the action for use with the activation statement; the behavior of such actions is described in the next chapter.

Statement syntax

statements ::= {statement ";"} statement
statement ::= "**skip**" | function-call | assignment | send
              | conditional | loop | activate

In any sequence of statements, the individual statements are separated by semicolons. The two fundamental statements are skip, which does nothing, and a function call, which invokes a C function and is more fully described on page 28.

assignment ::= left-sides ":=" expressions
left-sides ::= {left-side ","} left-side
left-side ::= (*id* | field-reference | array-reference)
expressions ::= {expression ","} expression

TAP assignment statements allow multiple values to be assigned simultaneously; in the code generated by the APC compiler, each expression is evaluated independently and stored in a temporary location. Subsequently, the values are assigned to the left-hand-side locations. Locations which can be assigned values are either variables, message fields, or array elements.

send ::= "**send**" m-name "**to**" address

A fundamental operation in TAP is sending a message, identified by m-name, to a process, identified by the address. Any necessary fields in the message should be set before executing the send statement.

conditional ::= "**if**" guarded-statements "**fi**"
guarded-statements ::= {guarded-statement "[]"} guarded-statement
guarded-statement ::= expression "->" statements

TAP provides a conditional statement with guarded branches separated by the box. Each branch consists of a boolean expression guarding a sequence of statements. In execution, one branch with a true-valued expression is chosen and executed. If no branches are enabled, execution continues with the next statement after the conditional.

loop ::= "**do**" expression "->" statements "**od**"

The iteration statement in TAP is made up of a single guarded statement, which provides a sequence of statements which are executed repeatedly as long as the expression evaluates to true.

activate ::= "**act**" t-name "**in**" delay
delay ::= expression

The activate statement, along with the timeout guards, is discussed in detail in Chapter 3. In general terms, it sets a timer associated with the timeout guard identified by t-name. The delay gives the value of the timer[3], after which the timeout guard enables the corresponding action.

---

[3] In milliseconds.

Expression syntax

In order to simplify the description of the TAP expression, the grammar rule is broken into a number of sub-rules below. The expression rule is the combination of all of the individual sub-rules.

expression ::= (*id* | *number* | **"true"** | **"false"** | *string*)

The fundamental expressions in TAP are variable names, numbers, true and false, and strings (which may only be used as arguments to function calls).

expression ::= field-reference
** | array-reference**
** | function-call**
field-reference ::= m-name "." (f-name | "size")
array-reference ::= (array-reference | *id*) "[" expression "]"
function-call ::= function-name "(" [expressions] ")"
function-name ::= *id*

Further expressions are field references, array references, and function calls. Field references are described by a message name and either a field within the message or the special field, "size", which contains the overall size of the message in bytes.

Array references follow the traditional syntax, with a numeric expressions describing the element within the array.

A function call identifies a C function by name and executes it with the arguments given by the expressions. The C type of the return value of the function should be one of:

- void, for functions called as statements,

- unsigned long, for integer values, or

- unsigned char *, for an assignment to a message's data field.

expression ::= "(" expression ")"
** | expression binary-operator expression**
** | unary-operator expression**

binary-operator ::= "=" | ">" | "<" "<=" | ">=" | "<>"
| "|" | "&" | "+" | "-" | "*" | "/"
unary-operator ::= "~" | "-"

The next group of general expressions include the normal binary and unary operators. The binary operators are equality, inequality, boolean operators, and arithmetic operators. Unary operators are boolean and arithmetic negation.

5   "=" ">" ">=" "<" "<=" "<>"
4   "&" "|"
3   "+" "-"
2   "*" "/"
1   "~" "-" (unary)

Figure 2.3: TAP operator precedence, from lowest to highest.

These operators have the precedence described in Figure 2.3.

expression ::= "size"

The final form of expression, a bare reference to a size message field, is only valid in an expression that is part of a message definition. The value of the "size" expression is the overall size of the message in bytes.

This page intentionally left blank

Chapter 3

EXECUTION MODELS OF NETWORK PROTOCOLS

An execution model for a programming notation describes the basic features of the computations for programs in the notation. These features include, for example, what information is captured at a state of the computation, what events can happen at each state, and the actual behavior of the events described in the notation.

With sequential languages, only one execution model is needed. A single execution model can support both:

- Effective reasoning about the program described in the notation, to produce both a clear, elegant design as well as arguments about the correct behavior of the program.

- Simple and efficient implementation of the program.

However, when the environment becomes more complex, as it does in the case of message-passing network protocols, a single model may not be sufficient. In fact, attempting to satisfy both goals in a single model may result in satisfying neither.

Two Models

This chapter presents two models for the execution of the Timed Abstract Protocol notation:

- The abstract model is intended to make protocol verification easy and to allow clear and elegant design. This model abstracts away many details of protocol execution and is not representative of reality.

- The concrete model is intended to be easily implemented, with no features that would be complex or inefficient to provide in a running system.

With two models, a single protocol has two meanings. This chapter describes the two models and the next two chapters demonstrate the relationship between the two models and show under what conditions they are equivalent.

Abstract Execution Model

The abstract execution model is intended to provide a conceptual framework for thinking about network protocols. Since the environment of network protocols is complex, it is necessary for an abstract model to make strong, unrealistic assumptions. The goals of these assumptions are to simplify reasoning about network protocols while still providing a useful model representing the network protocol environment.

Abstract protocol state

The state of a protocol in the abstract execution model consists entirely of:

- The values of the variables of every process in the protocol, and

- The contents of the channel between each pair of process.

In the abstract execution model, when the protocol begins execution, the values of the variables of the initial state of each process are given in the process definition and all of the channels are empty.

Abstract protocol execution

The computation of the protocol in the abstract model consists of a sequence of action executions, moving the protocol from one state to the next. The computation of a protocol proceeds under the following assumptions concerning atomicity, message propagation, and fairness:

- *Global atomicity:* Only one action is executed at a time. At each state, one action from all of the enabled actions in all of the processes in the protocol is nondeterministically chosen and executed.

- *Immediate message propagation:* When a message is sent, if it is the first message in the channel, then the receiving action for that message is enabled for execution at the next state.

- *Global fairness:* In computation consisting of an infinite number of states, if an action becomes enabled at a state then it is either disabled or chosen for execution at a subsequent state.

From these assumptions, the computation of the request/reply protocol of Figure 2.2 can be understood. At the initial state, readyp is true and the channels are empty, so p.1 is the only enabled action. That action sends a rqst message to process q, and sets readyp to false. At the second state, q.1 is the only enabled action, and this action receives the rqst message and responds with a rply message. At the third state, p.2 is the only enabled action, and it sets readyp to true, returning the protocol to the initial state. Computation continues in this fashion forever; see Figure 3.1.

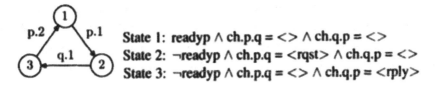

State 1: readyp ∧ ch.p.q = <> ∧ ch.q.p = <>
State 2: ¬readyp ∧ ch.p.q = <rqst> ∧ ch.q.p = <>
State 3: ¬readyp ∧ ch.p.q = <> ∧ ch.q.p = <rply>

Figure 3.1: State transitions for the request/reply protocol, version 1.

Unfortunately, the actual behavior of a network protocol is not this neat and the model so far presented is too unrealistic. At a minimum, it leaves out an important aspect of network protocol behavior: faults.

Abstract faults

The only faults described in the abstract execution model are message faults, which are the most common faults that network protocols must deal with. There are four possible message faults:

1. *Message loss:* A message in a channel is removed from the channel.

2. *Message corruption:* A message in a channel is replaced with the special message, *error,* which indicates that the message has been corrupted in some fashion.

3. *Message reordering:* The order of two messages in the same channel is swapped. A channel containing <m;n> subsequently contains <n;m>.

4. *Message duplication:* A message in a channel is duplicated. A channel containing <m> subsequently contains <m;m>.

The specific faults that a protocol may face depend on the environment in which the protocol executes. For example, if the protocol is intended to execute in an environment that provides message checksums, the possibility of message corruption is eliminated—a message corruption failure will be transformed into a message loss failure.

The message faults are treated almost identically to the other actions; if a channel contains a suitable message or messages, fault actions are enabled and can be chosen and executed. However, in a computation consisting of an infinite number of states, faults are *rare:* There can only be a finite number of faults.

With the addition of message faults, the request/reply protocol of Figure 2.2 has problems. On the one hand, the protocol need not deal with message re-ordering since the protocol has only one message in any channel at a time. Also, additional actions could be easily be added to the two processes to receive corrupt error messages and the protocol could be made to recognize duplicated messages by using message sequence numbers. On the other hand, if either the rqst or rply is lost, the protocol deadlocks. Each of the processes waits for a message that cannot arrive, and the TAP language as so far described provides no method of escaping this deadlock. The solution is the subject of the next section.

Abstract timeout behavior

In order to handle message loss, TAP has an additional action guard and an additional statement:

- The timeout guard, **timeout *t*,** provides a name, *t,* for the action. This name is used by the activation statement.

- The activation statement, **act *t* in *d*,** provides a delay, *d,* between the activation statement being executed and the timeout action *t* becoming enabled. For the request/reply protocol in this abstract model, the delay is essentially arbitrary—any non-zero delay will have the same behavior. However, in a protocol with multiple timeout actions or multiple delays, the delay values will describe the relative behavior of the timeouts.

Every timeout guard has a *time variable* associated with it, which either is null or has a numeric delay. Initially, the value of every time variable is null. The execution of an activation statement with a timeout guard name *t* sets the value of the time variable associated with the timeout guard *t* to the delay given in the activation statement.

At any abstract state where no action is enabled, the values of all of the non-null time variables are reduced by the value of the smallest non-null time variable, making the value of the smallest time variable or variables zero. A time variable with a zero value enables the associated timeout guard, and at a state where any time variable has a value of zero, only a timeout action can be executed. The execution of the timeout action resets its time variable to null.

```
process p
const q : address
var readyp : boolean = true
begin
    readyp  → send rqst to q;
                act rsnd in 1000;
                readyp := false
 | rcv rply from q  → readyp := true
 | timeout rsnd  → send rqst to q;
                act rsnd in 1000
end
```

Figure 3.2: Request/reply protocol, version 2.

Figure 3.2 shows process p with the addition of an activation statement and an action with a timeout guard. This version of the process, intended to handle message loss, executes an activation statement after sending a rqst, and the corresponding timeout action resends the rqst. Process q remains the same as in Figure 2.2.

In process p, the timeout delay used by the activation statements is 1000 ms, which must be an upper bound on the round-trip delay, by assumption. To avoid such assumptions, a protocol should simply choose the delay sensibly or dynamically adjust the delay, but will need to be prepared to handle duplicated messages.

Abstract execution of the request/reply protocol

The execution of the request/reply protocol of Figure 3.2 is more complex than the execution described on page 33. Figure 3.3 shows the state diagram of the protocol. In this diagram, State 1 represents situations where readyp is true and process p can send a rqst. States 2 and 3 represent situations with a message in one of the channels. State 4 represents situations where messages have been lost.

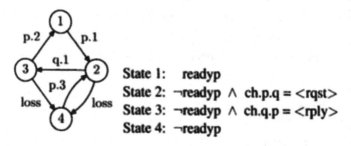

State 1: readyp
State 2: ¬readyp ∧ ch.p.q = <rqst>
State 3: ¬readyp ∧ ch.q.p = <rply>
State 4: ¬readyp

Figure 3.3: State transitions for the request/reply protocol, version 2. Channels not described are empty and transitions labelled "loss" represent message losses.

Process p from Figure 3.2 retransmits the rqst message when one is lost. At State 4, both ch.p.q and ch.q.p are empty and no actions are enabled. The time variable for the rsnd timeout action is reduced to zero and the timeout action is executed, resending the rqst message and returning the protocol to State 2.

Since a message could be lost again, it also re-executes the activation statement, resetting the time variable. In this execution in the abstract model, the specific value of the time variable for the rsnd timeout action, 1000, is not used; since it is the only time variable in the protocol, time passes in the abstract model of this protocol 1000 time unit jumps.

The slow request/reply protocol

Unfortunately, the request/reply protocol as described in Figure 3.2 violates the spirit, if not the letter, of protocol quiescence as described on page 19. As seen in Figure 3.3, the protocol overall never waits; as soon as a reply is received, the next request is sent. This is unrealistic because a continuous stream of requests, even if separated by replies, is not likely to be a worthwhile use of network resources.

A more realistic protocol is one which waits a given time between receiving a reply and sending the next request. This time is called the *delay*. Also, there is a period of time called *rtt;* a message loss has occurred if the rply is not received by process p within rtt time units of sending the rqst. Furthermore, for the moment we assume that rtt should be less than delay.

Figure 3.4 shows a modified version of process p of the request/reply that operates in this more realistic manner. Process q is unchanged from previous examples. An initial action activates the query timeout, sending the first rqst. Thereafter, p sends a rqst message delay time units after receiving the previous rply. If the rqst or rply is lost, the rsnd timeout action retransmits the rqst.

Figure 3.5 shows the state transition diagram for the slow request/reply protocol, assuming rtt < delay. The protocol begin execution in State 0. Normal execution proceeds from State 1 to State 2, by transmitting a rqst, then to State 3, by transmitting a rply, then to State 4, by receiving the rply, and back to State 1, by executing the rsnd timeout action. In the transition from State 4 to State 1, both the time variables for the query timeout action and the rsnd timeout action are non-null, but since rtt < delay, the retransmission will be checked before the next query can be sent. In this transition, the execution of p.3 does nothing, By the abstract timeout semantics, the time advanced between State 4 and State 2 (and hence the time taken in the normal loop of states) will be the delay, however.

```
process p
const q : address;
      delay : integer = 2000;
      rtt : integer = 1000;
var readyp : boolean = true
    initial : boolean = true
begin
      initial → act query in delay; initial := false
    | timeout query → send rqst to q;
                      readyp := false;
                      act rsnd in rtt
    | timeout rsnd → if ¬readyp → send rqst to q;
                                  act rsnd in rtt
                      | readyp → skip
                      fi
    | rcv rply from q → readyp := true; act query in delay
end
```

Figure 3.4: The slow request/reply protocol.

In the case that a message is lost, the process enters State 5, where no actions are enabled and the only non-null time variable is that for the rsnd timeout action, which will retransmit the rqst. Note that in a single rqst/rply exchange, the total time advanced between the previous rqst message and the next one will be delay plus rtt times the number of lost messages.

If we change our requirements so that rtt > delay, Figure 3.6 shows the state transition diagram of the protocol. The difference is the absence of State 4 between State 3 and State 1. The execution of action p.4, which receives the rply message, activates the query timeout guard with a value of delay. Since delay is less than rtt, action p.2 must be executed first, entering State 2.

Incidentally, in the case where rtt > delay, both the variable readyp and the conditional in p.3 are redundant: readyp will always be true when p.2 is executed and always be false when p.3 is executed. However, their presence does make the protocol more general across the values of rtt and delay.

Finally, if we alter the requirements so that rtt = delay, Figure 3.7 shows the state transition diagram. In this case, there is a race condition in State 4: both p.2 and p.3 can be executed. However, the execution of p.3 returns the protocol to State 1, while the execution of p.2 carries the protocol directly to

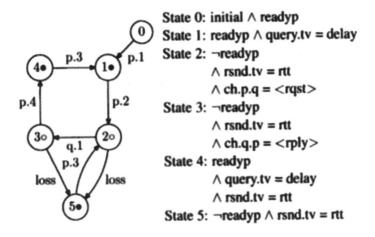

State 0: **initial ∧ readyp**
State 1: **readyp ∧ query.tv = delay**
State 2: **¬readyp**
 ∧ rsnd.tv = rtt
 ∧ ch.p.q = <rqst>
State 3: **¬readyp**
 ∧ rsnd.tv = rtt
 ∧ ch.q.p = <rply>
State 4: **readyp**
 ∧ query.tv = delay
 ∧ rsnd.tv = rtt
State 5: **¬readyp ∧ rsnd.tv = rtt**

Figure 3.5: State transitions for the slow request/reply protocol. In this figure, rtt < delay. States marked with o have non-null time variables and those marked with • have non-null time variables and no enabled actions. Time variables are indicated by rsnd.tv, where rsnd is the identifier of the timeout action guard. Time variables not described are null. Channels not described are empty. Transitions labelled "loss" represent message losses. The variable initial is false in all states except State 0.

State 2—p.2 resets the time variable for the rsnd timeout action.

As before, if generality across the values of rtt and delay is unimportant, the protocol can be altered to use only a single timeout, as shown in Figure 3.8. This timeout uses the value of readyp to determine whether to send a new request (if readyp is true) or to resend the previous request (if readyp is false). The resulting state transition diagram would resemble that in Figure 3.6.

Justification

The main goal of the abstract model is to provide a conceptually simple abstraction of the network protocol environment. The features of the abstract model combine to satisfy this goal:

1. Global atomicity and immediate message propagation limit the number of states that the model can be in, as well as the number of transitions between states.

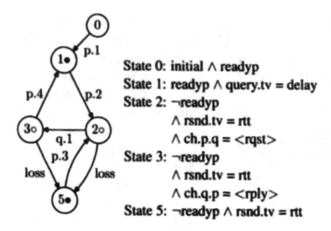

State 0: initial ∧ readyp
State 1: readyp ∧ query.tv = delay
State 2: ¬readyp
　　　∧ rsnd.tv = rtt
　　　∧ ch.p.q = <rqst>
State 3: ¬readyp
　　　∧ rsnd.tv = rtt
　　　∧ ch.q.p = <rply>
State 5: ¬readyp ∧ rsnd.tv = rtt

*Figure 3.6: State transitions for the slow request/reply protocol, where rtt >
delay. In State 1, either rsnd.tv = rtt or rsnd.tv is null, but since rtt > delay, both
cases behave the same—p.2 must be executed next.*

2. The model of message faults abstracts the general faults that a protocol
   may be subject to, retaining those that are realistically common.

3. The timeout behavior abstracts the passage of real time without reference to a clock. Again, this limits the number of states of the model.
   The timeout behavior also provides a flexible mechanism for describing
   protocols with time-based features.

4. Global fairness ensures progress in the protocol. If the correctness of
   the protocol requires the execution of a specific action and that action
   becomes enabled and is not subsequently disabled before it is executed,
   then it is guaranteed to eventually be executed.

The behavior of the abstract model described in this section is unrealistic,
but is *almost* reasonable. Another execution model, much closer to reality, is
described later. The relationship between the abstract model and the concrete
model, and the requirements made on protocols by that relationship, is the
subject of the next two chapters.

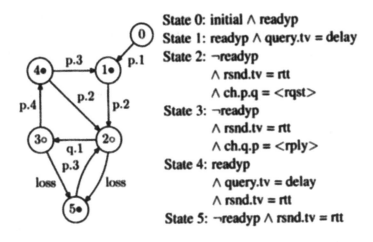

State 0: **initial ∧ readyp**

State 1: **readyp ∧ query.tv = delay**

State 2: **¬readyp**
  ∧ rsnd.tv = rtt
  ∧ ch.p.q = <rqst>

State 3: **¬readyp**
  ∧ rsnd.tv = rtt
  ∧ ch.q.p = <rply>

State 4: **readyp**
  ∧ query.tv = delay
  ∧ rsnd.tv = rtt

State 5: **¬readyp ∧ rsnd.tv = rtt**

Figure 3.7: State transitions for the slow request/reply protocol, where rtt =
delay.

[...]

| timeout qryrsnd → if readyp → send rqst to q;   /* Send new rqst */
  readyp := false
  | ¬readyp → send rqst to q   /* Resend last rqst */
  fi;
  act qryrsnd in rtt

[...]

Figure 3.8: Modifications to the slow request/reply protocol, where delay = rtt.
This action replaces actions p.2 and p.3 in Figure 3.4. Also, actions p.1 and p.4
need to be modified to activate qryrsnd rather than query.

Concrete Execution Model

Unlike the abstract execution model, the concrete execution model is designed to closely resemble the execution environment of a network protocol, including simultaneous events, delayed message propagation, clock-based timeouts, and local fairness.

As in the abstract execution model, when a protocol begins execution, the channels are empty and the values of the variables at the initial state of each process are given in the process definition. The computation also proceeds in a sequence of action executions.

Concrete protocol state

The state of a protocol in the concrete model has a more complex structure than that of the protocol in the abstract model. In addition to variables, each process has an *execution pointer,* which either indicates the next statement to be executed in an action of the process or takes a null value when no action is being executed by the process. Also, rather than consisting of a single queue, the channel between each pair of processes p and q is divided into two queues, an incoming queue of ch.p.q and an outgoing queue of ch.p.q. When a process p sends a message m to process q, message m is placed at the tail of the incoming queue of ch.p.q. Later, m is moved from the head of the incoming queue of ch.p.q to the tail of the outgoing queue of ch.p.q. Finally, process q receives m, removing it from the head of the outgoing queue.

Concrete protocol execution

The execution of the protocol is broken into *events*. Each event is one of:

1. An action choice. In this event, which is possible when a process has a null execution pointer and an enabled local or receive action guard, one enabled action of the process is nondeterministically chosen and the execution pointer of the process is set to the first statement of that action. If the chosen action has a receive guard, then this event also removes the message specified by the guard from the head of the outgoing queue of the channel.

2. The execution of a **skip** statement.

3. The execution of an assignment statement.

4. The execution of a send statement. In this event, the message is inserted into the incoming queue of the specified channel.

5. The execution of a timeout activation statement.

6. The execution of a conditional choice. This event is possible when the execution pointer points to either a conditional statement or an iteration statement. If the pointer points to a conditional statement, one branch is nondeterministically chosen from the enabled branches and the execution pointer is set to the first statement of that branch. If no branch is enabled, the execution pointer is set to the next statement in the action being executed. If the execution pointer points to an iteration statement and the iteration guard is true, the execution pointer is set to the first statement of the iteration body. Otherwise, the execution pointer is set to the next statement in the action being executed or to null, if the conditional is the final statement of the action.

7. A fault occurance.

8. A message transmission. In this event, a message is moved from the head of the incoming queue of a channel to the tail of the outgoing queue of the same channel.

9. A timer advance. Timeout behavior in the concrete model is described on page 46. However, the timer advance event possibly sets the execution pointer of one or more processes to the first statement of an action with a timeout guard; in this case, it also sets the time variable associated with the action to null.

Events 1 -6 are executed in some process in TAP. Events 2, 3, 4 and 5 set the execution pointer of the process to the next statement in the action being executed. When one of these events is the final statement of an action, the execution pointer is set to null.

A concrete computation of the protocol consists of a sequence of steps moving the protocol from one state to the next, starting with the initial state of the protocol. A *step* in a concrete computation consists of one or more simultaneous events such that, for any two events e_1 and e_2 occurring in the same step, the following conditions hold:

1. *Process execution.* There are six types of events describing the execution of actions in a process:

   (a) Choosing an action, Event 1.

   (b) Executing a **skip,** Event 2.

   (c) Executing an assignment, Event 3.

   (d) Sending a message, Event 4.

   (e) Activating a timeout, Event 5.

   (f) Evaluating a conditional choice, Event 6.

   If e_1 is one of these events for some action in a process, then e_2 cannot be one of these events for any action in the same process.

2. *Action choice.* If e_1 is an action choice event, Event 1, in some process, then the execution pointer of that process at the concrete state immediately before the step is null.

3. *Action execution.* There are five types of events describing the execution of statements of an action in a process:

   (a) Executing a **skip,** Event 2.

   (b) Executing an assignment, Event 3.

   (c) Sending a message, Event 4.

   (d) Activating a timeout, Event 5.

   (e) Evaluating a conditional choice, Event 6.

   If e_1 is one of these events for some statement in an action in a process, then the execution pointer of that process at the state immediately before the step points to that statement.

4. *Message operation.* There are four types of events operating on a message:

    (a) Sending a message, Event 4.

    (b) Transmitting a message, Event 8.

    (c) Choosing an action which receives a message, Event 1.

    (d) A fault occurrence on a message, Event 7.

If e_1 is one of these events, e_2 cannot be one of these events operating on the same message.

5. *Message transmission.* If e_1 is a message transmission event in some channel, Event 8, then e_2 cannot be another message transmission event in the same channel.

6. *Timer advance.* A timer advance event, Event 9, cannot occur in a step with any other event.

The concrete execution model can be described as *locally atomic,* since the actions within each process are executed atomically. However, different processes execute in parallel, and many events can occur in the same step.

Delayed message propagation

The channels between processes are separated into two queues. When a message is sent from process p to process q, the message enters the *incoming* queue of channel ch.p.q, where it does not enable a receive action in process q even if it is the first message in the channel. A separate event, a *message transmission,* is needed to move the message from the incoming queue of ch.p.q to the *outgoing* queue of the same channel. When a message is at the head of the outgoing queue of ch.p.q, then the corresponding receive guard is enabled.

Concrete faults

The concrete model includes all of the faults listed on page 33: message loss, message corruption, message reordering, and message duplication.

    For simplicity, all faults in the concrete execution model occur when the message suffering the fault is in the outgoing queue of the channel. (There is no loss of generality in this requirement, since any fault in the incoming queue before the message is transmitted is equivalent to the same fault in the outgoing queue, after the message has been transmitted.)

Concrete timeout behavior

The concrete execution model includes the timeout activation statement and the timeout guard as described on page 34, with the activation statement behaving exactly as in the abstract execution model. However, the concrete model includes an event called a timer advance, Event 9, which is allowed whenever a time variable is non-null at any state where the execution pointers of all processes are null. Each timer advance reduces the values of all non-null time variables by one; if any time variable becomes zero, then the timer advance resets the time variable to null and sets the execution pointer of the process with the associated timeout action to the first statement of the timeout action.

Local fairness

In the concrete execution model, execution is *locally fair:* In a computation consisting of an infinite number of states,

1. If an action in a given process becomes enabled, eventually either that process will execute the action or the action will be disabled.

2. A message in the incoming queue of a channel will eventually be transmitted to the outgoing queue.

This condition differs from the global fairness condition in that it only describes the execution within a single process, not throughout the network protocol.

Concrete execution of the request/reply protocol

The flavor of the execution of the request/reply protocol can be found in the sequence of steps in Figure 3.9. Each line horizontally represents a step; the left column shows events in the execution of process p and the right column shows events in the execution of process q. Each event in the figure is followed by the identifying number of the event in parentheses. The first four steps show the execution of the action from process p guarded by readyp. The next three steps show two timer advances and the transmission of the request message in ch.q.p. The next two steps show the execution of the action of process q. The next step shows the transmission of the reply message in ch.q.p. The final two steps show the execution of the receive action of process p.

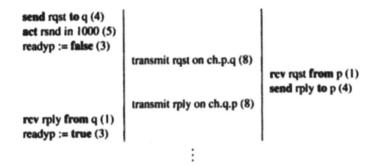

Figure 3.9: Computation steps for request/reply protocol. Each line horizontally represents a step; the left column shows events in the execution of process p and the right column shows events in the execution of process q.

Justification

The concrete execution model is designed to represent the normal execution environment of an asynchronous, message passing network protocol. It does so in the following ways:

- Local atomicity models the execution of a group of processes: each process serially executes its actions, but multiple processes execute in parallel.

- The channels between processes can take an arbitrary time to deliver a message, even with no faults.

- Local fairness allows a computation to delay an action with a enabled local predicate indefinitely by executing other enabled actions. On the other hand, message and timeouts are acted on fairly.

Clearly, the concrete execution model differs from the abstract execution model. However, the two execution models can be shown to be equivalent for a rich class of protocols. This equivalence is discussed in the next chapter.

This page intentionally left blank

Chapter 4

EQUIVALENCE OF EXECUTION MODELS

The relationship between the abstract and concrete models is one of *implementation:* the abstract model of a protocol P in TAP represents the specification of P whereas the concrete model of P represents its implementation.

This relationship is complex. On the one hand, they share the same notation and fundamental operations, but on the other, they have different operational assumptions. Fortunately, the two models are equivalent for a large class of protocol computations. In other words, it is possible to demonstrate that a protocol that behaves correctly in the abstract model will also behave correctly in the concrete model, and vice versa.

In order to demonstrate the equivalence of the abstract execution model from page 32 and the concrete execution model from page 42, a number of terms and relationships first need to be defined.

Protocol states

The state of a protocol in a model describes all of the useful information about the protocol at a point in its computation, specifically determining the next transitions that are possible.

An *abstract state* of a protocol in the abstract execution model is:

- The values of all variables in all processes in the protocol, and

- The contents of all channels between processes in the protocol.

A *concrete state* of a protocol in the concrete execution model is:

- The values of all variables in all processes in the protocol,

- The values of the execution pointers of all processes in the protocol, and

- The contents of all incoming and outgoing queues of channels between processes in the protocol.

For convenience, we adopt the notation that abstract states are named *as,* *at,* and so on, whereas concrete states are named *cs, ct,* and so on. When discussing corresponding states, a hub state *cs* corresponds to an abstract state *as,* a hub state *ct* corresponds to an abstract state *at,* and so on.

In the concrete execution model, the *extent* of an event consists of the variables, execution pointers, and messages in the concrete states before and after the step with the event. Specifically,

1. The extent of an action choice event, Event 1, consists of the variables and execution pointer of the process executing the event, and the messages at the head of the outgoing queues of the channels terminating with the process.

2. The extent of a **skip** event, Event 2, consists of the execution pointer of the process executing the event.

3. The extent of an assignment event, Event 3, consists of the variables and execution pointer of the process executing the event.

4. The extent of a send event, Event 4, consists of the execution pointer of the process executing the send statement and the message being inserted into the incoming queue of a channel.

5. The extent of a timeout activation event, Event 5, consists of the execution pointer of the process executing the activation statement and the time variable associated with the timeout guard being activated.

6. The extent of a conditional choice event, Event 6, consists of the variables and execution pointer of the process executing the event.

7. The extent of a fault occurrence, Event 7, consists of the message or messages altered or destroyed by the event.

8. The extent of a message transmission, Event 8, is the message being transmitted.

9. The extent of a timer advance event, Event 9, consists of all of the existing time variables and the execution pointers of the processes containing those time variables.

Further, two events in the concrete execution model are *independent* if and only if the extents of the two events do not overlap, in which case the events do not observe or modify the same variables, time variables, process execution pointers, or messages.

Equivalent protocol states

A concrete state is a *hub state* if and only if:

- The values of the execution pointers of all processes in the state are null.

- The incoming queue of each channel in the state is empty.

Informally, every hub state corresponds to some abstract state. At a hub state in a computation of some protocol, the next event in the execution of every process will be to begin an action, and since every message in a channel is in the outgoing queue of the channel, the actions that are enabled are the same as in the corresponding abstract state.

An abstract state, *as*, and a corresponding concrete state, *cs*, of the same protocol are *equivalent* if and only if the following conditions hold:

- *cs* is a hub state.

- The values of the variables in *as are* equal to the values of the variables in *cs*.

- The sequence of messages in the outgoing queue of each channel in *cs* is identical to the sequence of messages in the corresponding channel in *as*.

Every abstract state is equivalent to some hub state, but not every concrete state is equivalent to an abstract state; in particular, the non-hub states are not equivalent to any abstract state.

State transitions

An *abstract transition* is a pair of abstract states, *as* and *at,* such that there is an action or error enabled at *as* and the execution of this action or the occurrence of this error leads to *at.*

A *concrete transition* is a pair of concrete states, *cs* and *ct,* such that there is a step consisting of one or more events each allowed at *cs* and the simultaneous execution of the step leads to *ct.*

Computations

An *abstract computation* of a protocol is a possibly infinite sequence of abstract states of the protocol beginning with the initial state of the protocol, such that every pair of successive states is an abstract transition.

A *concrete computation* of a protocol is a possibly infinite sequence of concrete states of the protocol beginning with the initial state of the protocol, such that every pair of successive states is a concrete transition.

Whole computations

It is possible to have a concrete computation that cannot be related to an abstract computation simply because, at every state of the concrete computation, some action is always in the process of being executed; in other words, an execution pointer of at least one process is non-null at each state of the concrete computation. In such a computation, there are no hub states after the initial state. Also, since timer advance events are allowed in any concrete state where all of the execution pointers are null, it is possible to have a concrete computation where timeouts happen too fast: where every time variable is reduced to zero immediately after it is created and the associated timeout action is executed before it would be in the abstract model.

However, a class of finite concrete computations, called whole computations, can be defined so that any concrete computation in this class *can* be related to a finite abstract computation. A *whole computation* is a finite concrete computation in which:

1. The final state of the concrete computation is a hub state.

2. Only hub states with no enabled action guards are the initial states of transitions with timer advance events.

While both of these requirements are chosen for technical reasons, they do have intuitive justifications. For the first requirement, a final hub state for any finite concrete computation can be identified by appending the remaining events from the incomplete action executions as well as the message transmission events for the messages in the incoming queue of any channel. For the second requirement, if the amount of time described by a timer advance is greater than the duration of the execution of an action, it is reasonable to assume that the processes execute each enabled action without delays. As a result, the protocol spends most of its running time waiting.

Equivalent computations

Let P be a protocol specified in TAP, P_A be a finite abstract computation of P, and P_C be a whole concrete computation of P.

The two computations P_A and P_C are *equivalent* if and only if:

1. The final state of P_A is equivalent to the final state of P_C.

2. The sequence of actions and faults executed in P_A is the same as the sequence of actions and faults executed in P_C.

   Since actions in the concrete execution model are not atomic, for an action to be executed in P_C means that the events making up the execution of the action are executed in sequence in P_C.

The two requirements indicate that equivalent computations end equivalently, and in the process of execution behave equivalently.

Proof of equivalence

In order to demonstrate that the abstract execution model and the concrete execution model are equivalent, we will prove that the models satisfy the following two conditions for any protocol P specified in TAP that satisfies the conditions we have described:

1. *Implementation consistency:* For any whole concrete computation P_C, there exists an equivalent finite abstract computation P_A.

2. *Implementation completeness:* For any finite abstract computation P_A, there exists an equivalent finite concrete computation P_C. (It will turn out that P_C is whole.)

Figure 4.1 presents a graphical representation of the two conditions. The set A is made up of finite abstract computations of protocol P and the set C is made up of whole concrete computations of P.

Implementation completeness

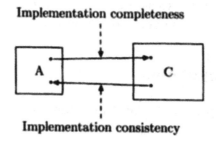

Implementation consistency

Figure 4.1: The execution model relationship. A is the set of finite abstract computations of protocol P specified in TAP and C is the set of whole concrete computations for P.

In the next section, we prove that the implementation consistency condition holds, and in the following section we prove that the implementation completeness condition holds.

Implementation consistency

In this section, we demonstrate that the implementation consistency condition holds by transforming the whole concrete computation P_C of a protocol P specified in TAP into an equivalent concrete computation P_C' of P, which is itself equivalent to an abstract computation P_A of P. P_C' is constructed from P_C by *serialization* and *reordering*.

Event serialization

The computation P_C of a process P specified in TAP consists of a sequence of transitions, where each transition is a step made up of one or more events. The first transformation serializes each step of P_C, resulting in a computation consisting of a sequence of transitions made up of single events. Fortunately, this transformation is possible because simultaneous events in the concrete execution model are independent.

Theorem 1 *Any two events that occur in the same step of a concrete computation of a protocol are independent.*

Proof
Let e_1 and e_2 be two events that occur in the same step of P_C.

- If e_1 is an event in the execution of an action, e_2 must not be an event in the execution of an action from the same process by the process execution condition described on page 44, Rule 1. Since the execution model does not allow shared variables, they cannot observe or modify the same variables, time variables, or execution pointer.

- If e_1 is an event operating on a message, e_2 cannot operate on the same message, by the message operations condition, Rule 4.

- If e_1 is a message transmission, e_2 cannot also be a transmission on the same channel, by the message transmission condition, Rule 5.

Therefore, e_1 and e_2 cannot observe or modify the same variables, time variables, execution pointers, or messages, and e_1 and e_2 are independent.
∎

Given that any two events in the same step are independent, a step consisting of more than one event can be transformed into a sequence of steps.

Theorem 2 (Serialization) *A step consisting of n simultaneous events, where $n > 1$, can be converted to a sequence of two steps, the first consisting of one event and the second consisting of $n - 1$ events, such that if the original step starts at state cs and yields state ct, and if the sequence starts at state cs, then the sequence will also yield state ct. (See Figure 4.2.)*

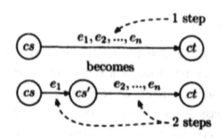

Figure 4.2: The serialization transformation.

Proof

Consider two transitions:

- A concrete transition made up of a step consisting of events $e_1, e_2, ...e_n$ beginning in *cs* and ending in *ct*, and

- A sequence of two transitions beginning in *cs*, the first transition made up of a step consisting of e_1 and ending in *cs'*, and the second transition beginning in *cs'* and made up of a step consisting of $e_2, ...e_n$ and ending in *ct'*.

By Theorem 1, e_1 must be independent of all of $e_2...e_n$. Therefore, all of the extents of $e_2...e_n$ remain unchanged from *cs* to *cs'* in the sequence and the extent of e_1 remains unchanged from *cs'* to *ct'* in the sequence by $e_2...e_n$. Therefore, *ct'* is equivalent to *ct*.

∎

Let P_C^s be the concrete computation constructed by repeatedly serializing the transitions in P_C, such that all transitions in P_C^s consist of steps of a single event.

1. Since the serialization transformation only introduces states, all of the states in P_C occur in P_C^s in order, although they may be separated by intermediate states.

2. All of the events in P_C occur in P_C^s, and those events which are not simultaneous in P_C occur in the same order.

3. For all of the events in any transition of P_C, the extent of the event is equal to the extent of the same event in P_C^s.

For the remainder of this chapter, we consider only this serialized computation P_C^s.

Event reordering

The serialized concrete computation P_C^s consists of a sequence of transitions made up of single-event steps, where the events from the execution of an action in one process can be interleaved with the events from the execution of actions from other processes and with faults. The second transformation reorders the steps of P_C^s to produce an equivalent computation which is itself equivalent to an abstract computation.

A serialized concrete computation is *uninterrupted* if the following conditions hold:

1. **Abstract action atomicity.** All steps with events in the execution of an action (Events 1, 2, 3, 4, 5, and 6) are not separated by any steps with events from the execution of any other action, faults (Event 7), or timer advances (Event 9).

2. **Abstract message transmission.** Every event sending a message (Event 4) is immediately followed by the message transmission event (Event 8) for that message.

3. **Abstract timer advance.** The timer advance event reducing a time variable to zero occurs only in a hub state where all other actions are disabled.

The goal of reordering is to construct an uninterrupted concrete computation P_C' from a serialized concrete computation P_C^s.

In order to transform the serialized computation P_C^s into an uninterrupted computation P_C', the initial event in each action execution is held fixed in the sequence and the remaining events in the execution of every action are moved left to be sequential with the preceding events in the execution of the action.

Theorem 3 (Reordering) *A sequence of two concrete transitions, each consisting of a single event where the two events are independent, can be reordered such that if the original sequence starts at state* cs *and yields state* cu, *and if*

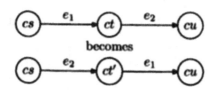

Figure 4.3: The reordering transformation.

the new sequence starts at state cs, then the new sequence will also yield cu.
(See Figure 4.3.)

Proof

Let e_1 be the event making up a transition beginning in *cs* and yielding *ct,* and
e_2 be an event making up the transition beginning in *ct* and yielding *cu*. If e_1
is independent of e_2, then the extent of e_2 is unchanged by e_1 from *cs* to *ct,*
and therefore it is possible to create a transition made up of e_2 from *cs* to a new
state *ct'*. Since e_1 is independent of e_2, the extent of e_1 remains unchanged
from *cs* to *ct'* and therefore it is possible to create a second transition made up
of e_1 from *ct'* to a new state *cu'*. However, the extent of e_2 remains unchanged
from *ct'* to *cu'*, and therefore, *cu'* is equivalent to *cu*.
■

The new sequence from *cs* to *cu* replaces the original sequence in the computation. In order to use the reordering theorem, the events which are independent must be identified.

Theorem 4 *Events in an execution of an action (2, 3, 4, 5, and 6) are independent of:*

1. *Prior events in the computation which are part of the execution of actions
   in other processes.*

2. *Message transmission events unless the first event sends the message
   which is transmitted.*

3. *Fault events unless the first event sends the message which suffers the
   fault.*

Proof

Let e_1 be one of Events 2, 3, 4, 5, or 6 of an execution of an action in process p.

1. Let e_2 be one of Events 1,2,3, 4, 5, or 6 of an execution of an action in process q, where $p \neq q$. The extent of e_1 includes only variables of p, the execution pointer of p, and time variables for actions of p, and messages in the incoming queue of channels originating at p. Likewise, the extent of e_2 includes only variables of q, the execution pointer of q, and time variables for actions of q, and message in the incoming queue of channels originating at q, or in the outgoing queue of channels terminating at q. Since these extents do not overlap, e_1 and e_2 are independent.

2. Let e_2 be a message transmission event (Event 8) for a message m.

   - If e_1 is not a send event, then its extent does not include a message. Therefore, e_1 and e_2 are independent.
   - If e_1 is a send event for a message m' and $m \neq m'$, then since e_1 and e_2 do not operate on the same message, e_1 and e_2 are independent.

   As a result, e_1 and e_2 are independent.

3. Let e_2 be a fault event (Event 7) on a message m. By reasoning similar to the case above, e_1 and e_2 are independent.

◼

Theorem 4 enables the construction of a concrete computation that follows the abstract action atomicity condition from P_C^s.

Theorem 5 *A serialized concrete computation containing a transition made up of an event from the execution of an action following another transition made up of an event from the same execution of the action can be reordered so that the second event immediately follows the first.*

Proof

Let e_1 and e_2 be concrete transitions in P_C^s that are part of a single execution of an action, where e_2 follows e_1.

- e_1 is one of Events 1, 2, 3, 4, 5, or 6.

- e_2 is one of Events 2, 3, 4, 5, or 6.

If e_1 and e_2 are separated by other events, each of these intervening events must be one of:

1. Events 1, 2, 3, 4, 5, or 6 in the execution of other processes. However, e_2 can be reordered with such an event, because by Theorem 4, the events are independent.

2. Fault events (7) or message transmission events (8) that do not involve messages also involved in the transition being reordered. Again, by Theorem 4, e_2 can be reordered with such an event, since even if e_2 sends a message, it cannot be the one transmitted.

The intervening event cannot be a timer advance event (9), since timer advance events are assumed to only occur in hub states and there is no hub state between e_1 and e_2. Therefore, the computation can be reordered to make e_1 and e_2 immediately sequential.

■

In order to achieve the abstract message transmission condition, we must demonstrate that reordering P_C^s to follow the abstract message transmission condition is possible.

Theorem 6 *A serialized concrete computation can be reordered so that a transition with a message transmission event immediately follows the transition with the event sending the message, as long as send or message transmission events involving messages in the same channel.*

Proof

As described on page 45, any fault events involving a message only occur after the message is transmitted from the incoming queue of the channel to the outgoing queue. Likewise, the action choice event removing the message from the channel occurs after the message is transmitted. Therefore, a message transmission must be independent of any intervening events between the event sending the message and the transmission event. By Theorem 3, the transition with the transmission event can be reordered with any such intervening transition.

∎

Following Theorem 5 and Theorem 6, it becomes possible to construct the uninterrupted concrete computation.

Theorem 7 *A serialized concrete computation P_C^s can be converted into an uninterrupted concrete computation.*

Proof

The uninterrupted computation can be constructed by first noting that the first transition in the computation is an action choice event, the first event in the execution of an action, and then following the algorithm:

1. Reorder the computation so that the current action follows the abstract action atomicity condition. (Theorem 5.)

2. If the current action sends any messages, reorder the computation so that this action follows the abstract message transmission condition. The reordering must be done for each message sent by the action in the order that the messages are sent, to preserve the order of the messages in the channel. (Theorem 6.)

3. The state following the current action is a hub state. If there are no further transitions in the computation, the uninterrupted computation has been completed. If there are further transitions, the next transition from this hub state is one of the following:

   - A timer advance not setting the execution pointer of any process, or a fault event. In this case, the next state is also a hub state; continue with step 3 while examining the next transition.

   - A timer advance setting the execution pointer of one or more processes. In this case, reorder the computation so that each action execution initiated by the timer advance follows the abstract atomicity and abstract message transmission conditions. Then, continue with step 3 following the final transition in the last of the actions.

- An action choice event. In this case, continue with step 1.

Because the reorderings described by Theorem 5 and Theorem 6 do not alter hub states, timer advance events are not involved in these reorderings. As a result, timer advance events remain unaltered in the new computation and because the original computation was whole, it therefore satisfies the abstract timer advance condition.

The algorithm terminates, because it traverses the computation from beginning to end, and when it does, the reordered computation is uninterrupted.

∎

The uninterrupted computation P'_C constructed by the steps above is equivalent to an abstract computation.

Theorem 8 (Implementation consistency) *For any whole concrete computation of a protocol specified in TAP, there exists an equivalent finite abstract computation of the protocol.*

Proof

Let P_C be a concrete computation of a protocol P specified in TAP and P'_C be an uninterrupted computation produced from P_C by the steps above. P'_C is equivalent to some finite abstract computation P_A because:

- The final state of P_C is a hub state, which is preserved in P'_C. This state is equivalent to the final state of P_A.

- An uninterrupted computation consists of a sequence of:

  – Serial events representing the execution of an action followed by a hub state.

  – Fault transitions, followed by a hub state.

  – Timer advance events, followed by either a hub state or the execution of an action. The timer advance events obey the same conditions as the abstract timeout semantics; specifically, that actions with timeout guards only become enabled when no other guard is enabled and that all timeout actions with enabled guards are executed before any non-timeout action which may become enabled.

As a result, the sequence of actions and faults executed in P'_C are the same as that in P_A.

∎

Implementation completeness

As described previously, implementation completeness means that, for any finite abstract computation of a protocol P, there exists an equivalent finite concrete computation. The concrete computation is constructed using the abstract computation as a model.

Theorem 9 *For any finite abstract computation of a protocol specified in TAP, there exists an equivalent finite concrete computation of the protocol.*

Proof
Let P_A be a finite abstract computation of a protocol P specified in TAP. Construct P_C from P_A by doing the following:

1. Begin with a sequence of concrete hub states, where each hub state in the sequence is equivalent to the corresponding abstract state in P_A.

2. Between each pair of hub states corresponding to an action execution abstract transition, insert a sequence of concrete transitions consisting of single events corresponding to the execution of the action.

3. Immediately following each send event, insert a message transmission event for the message.

4. Insert a concrete transition consisting of an error event between each pair of hub states corresponding to an abstract fault.

5. Immediately prior to the execution of an event choosing a timeout action, insert a number of steps consisting of timer advance events equal to the value of the time variable associated with the action.

The resulting P_C is equivalent to P_A, since

- By the first step, the final state of P_C is equivalent to the final state of P_A.

- By the second and fourth steps, the sequence of action executions and faults in P_C is the same as the sequence in P_A.

Also, the resulting P_C is a valid concrete computation of P, since every pair of successive states is a concrete transition—the second and fourth steps fill the transitions between all of the hub states and the third and fifth steps ensure that the correct actions are enabled at the next hub state.

■

Related work

The proofs in this chapter (and the next) have antecedents, especially in considering the atomicity of distributed systems.

Sivilotti[47] describes a set of conditions under which sections of code can be considered atomic without explicit care to ensure their atomicity, simplifying reasoning about distributed systems. Conveniently, message passing systems such as those described here in the concrete model satisfy those conditions as long as a message can experience only a finite delay. As will be seen in the next chapter, the fairness condition of the concrete model ensures this property.

Lipton[48] proved a theorem concerning combining atomic operations to demonstrate partial correctness and deadlock-freedom properties, using commutivity relations between atomic actions in a manner that appears to be similar to that of this chapter.

Lamport and Schneider[49] and Lamport[50] also discuss the demonstration of safety properties for a program if the properties hold for a coarser-grained but otherwise similar program. However, the relationship between Lamport's work and the two models described here is clearer in the latter. In that paper, Lamport characterizes the relationship between a distributed algorithm $\mathcal{A}$ (analogous to a protocol executed in the concrete model) and a reduced version of the same algorithm, $\hat{\mathcal{A}}$ (analogous to a protocol executed in the abstract model), in which "an entire operation is a single atomic action and message transmission is instantaneous." The conditions Lamport gives for this reduction to hold are satisfied by the abstract and concrete models, along with the protocol style assumptions in Chapter 2.

By satisfying the conditions of the previous work, any results due to those theorems apply to the relationship between the abstract and concrete models. In fact, the proofs in this chapter and the next could be considered to be corollaries of the previous theorems, although corollaries limited to the TAP asynchronous message-passing system. However, the proofs in this chapter and the next go further by asserting an equivalence between the two models. This equivalence is not limited to properties relying on atomicity, and relates the models in both directions.

This page intentionally left blank

Chapter 5

PRESERVING FAIRNESS

The previous chapter dealt with the equivalence of the two models of execution based on finite computations. This equivalence indicates that the two models are strongly related. However, one aspect of the two models that was not dealt with by the previous chapter is fairness, since fairness does not apply to finite computations. This chapter describes the relationship between global and local fairness for infinite computations.

Because in both models fairness is described in terms of action executions, this chapter will deal with a simplified version of the concrete model which is identical to the abstract model except for the local fairness condition. As a result, all states described are abstract states, and the events of the concrete model are not mentioned. Also, since the abstract model does not feature delayed message propagation, local fairness is projected into the abstract model by removing the condition requiring eventual message transmission. Similar arguments can be made in the concrete model by constructing a projection of global fairness, but the proofs would be more complex.

Global fairness

An infinite abstract computation is *globally fair* if, when an action in any process becomes enabled in a state as_i, then the computation has a subsequent state $as_j, j \geq i$, where that action is either disabled or executed.

Local fairness

An infinite abstract computation is *locally fair* if, when an action in process p is enabled in a state as_i, then the computation has a subsequent state $as_j, j \geq i$, where that action is either disabled or executed.

Global fairness differs from local fairness in that the former is property of the global computation while the latter is a property of each process in a computation.

Proof of fairness equivalence

The proof that global and local fairness are equivalent is presented in two steps: first, that global fairness implies local fairness for abstract computations, and second, that local fairness implies global fairness for abstract computations.

Theorem 10 *Any globally fair abstract computation is locally fair.*

Proof

Let P_G be a globally fair abstract computation of protocol P specified in TAP, p be a process in P, and $p.l$ be an action of p that is enabled in state as_i of P_G. By global fairness, there is a state $as_j, j \geq i$, where $p.l$ is disabled or executed. In either case, P_G satisfies the conditions for local fairness.
∎

Theorem 11 *Any locally fair abstract computation is globally fair.*

Proof

Let P_L be a locally fair computation of protocol P specified in TAP, p be a process in P, and $p.l$ be an action of p that is enabled in state as_i of P_L. By local fairness, there is a state $as_j, j \geq i$, where $p.l$ is disabled or executed. Therefore, P_L satisfies the conditions for global fairness.
∎

Fairness and the Austin Protocol Compiler

As described previously, local fairness is a property of each process in a computation. As a result, assuming the statements in each action of the process are well behaved as described in Chapter 2, it is possible for the compiler and runtime environment to ensure local fairness for individual processes while a guarantee of global fairness would be impractical. Specifically, as long as each action execution terminates, the APC system will ensure that an action which becomes enabled will not be ignored forever; it will eventually either be executed or become disabled.

Early versions of the Austin Protocol Compiler did not make this guarantee, as they used a different algorithm for choosing actions to attempt to execute. The necessity of the guarantee did not become clear until attempting to create the proofs in this chapter—the original proofs were more complex and made significant requirements of protocols in order to preserve fairness—and the implementation of the guarantee required changes in the compiler and the runtime system. It is interesting to note that the subsequent algorithm for choosing actions is much simpler than the original; the changes brought on to improve the fairness qualities also improved the implementation.

A similar situation also occurred regarding the timeout semantics described in Chapter 3. The early versions of the APC system allowed multiple time variables for each timeout action. The proofs in the previous chapter, as well as the realization that the current approach made many protocols simpler, brought on a change to a single time variable per timeout action, and the implementation of that change improved the compiler and runtime system.

The next chapter contains a detailed examination of the current APC system.

This page intentionally left blank

Chapter 6

THE AUSTIN PROTOCOL COMPILER

The final piece of the protocol development puzzle is the Austin Protocol Compiler, or APC, which can transform a process described in TAP into executable code in C. In use, the philosophy behind APC is similar to that of yacc—to provide a simple, flexible interface to complex underlying techniques. Within this philosophy, a protocol specification is written in TAP, based on the abstract execution model. APC then translates that specification into an executable system, based on the concrete execution model.

The most important requirement for APC is to correctly implement the concrete execution model of the TAP notation. Some parts of this requirement are necessarily assumptions made about the execution environment and others are implemented by the systems on which APC is based, but the major component of the requirement must be dealt with by the APC implementation. Additionally, there are two further goals for APC:

- Integration with the C systems programming language. TAP, the language provided by APC, is necessarily simple and by design does not contain many features necessary to a general-purpose programming language. Rather than extending this language, APC provides for protocols to call arbitrary C functions, allowing file input/output, cryptography, database and buffer management, and other tasks to be handled in the manner best suited for each of them.

- Simplicity of implementation. Before APC can meet any other goals, its correct operation must be assured. By keeping the implementation simple and the compiler's output understandable, this assurance can be validated.

APC generates portable C code as shown in Figure 6.1. The file containing the TAP source is *filename.ap,* the file *filename.c* contains function definitions,

Figure 6.1: The Austin Protocol Compiler

and the file *filename.h* contains the data structure definitions and function prototypes.

The generated code is intended to be readable and uses meaningful identifiers based on the original TAP source. This choice does have a disadvantage
in that the identifiers may conflict with those used elsewhere by the programmer, however it provides the advantage of allowing the generated code to be
compared with the original source.

Error handling in APC is currently somewhat primitive, with some errors
only identified by the C compiler. Fortunately, the readability of the generated
code and the structural similarity of the code to the original source make these
errors significantly easier to locate.

The APC runtime library is built on top of a base network protocol, which
provides services for sending and receiving messages. The base network protocol supported by the current version is UDP. In turn, the APC-generated code
interfaces with other systems for specific functionality within the control structure of the protocol.

The remainder of this chapter discusses the architecture of the Austin
Protocol Compiler, the programming interfaces provided by the compiler-
generated code and the runtime library, and the details of the runtime library
itself.

Architecture of the compiler

The compiler is implemented in approximately 1500 lines of Python plus a
500 line grammar specification using Flex and Bison and a 1000 line C/Python
interface between the parser and the Python code.[1] The overall architecture of
the compiler is shown in Figure 6.2. The Python components of the compiler

---

[1]This interface, made up of two components called FlexModule and BisonModule, is a separate, generic package.

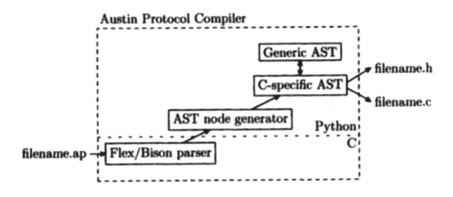

Figure 6.2: Architecture of APC.

are written in an object-oriented fashion, with the primary classes being nodes of the abstract syntax tree. The AST is instantiated by the AST node generator of Figure 6.2, called from the parser. The generic AST nodes, part of the Generic AST in Figure 6.2, are instances of classes for tokens and symbols. These instances provide access to the information from the parse tree such as identifier names, numeric values, and sub-trees. The base module containing the AST generator and the generic AST classes also provides the interface to call the parser on a file, as well as syntax and other error handling.

A second module provides C code generation. This module consists of subclasses of the generic AST node classes, shown as the C-specific AST in Figure 6.2. These subclasses provide methods to the generate C code from their corresponding elements of the abstract syntax of TAP.

The compiler design is simple, compact, and provides the ability to further extend the C code generator or to replace it with other output generators.

The code generated by the compiler is made up of two major pieces: message handling and TAP processes.

Message handling

In the generated C code, messages are represented by three components:

1. A data structure named after the message, describing the message's fields for use in the process' actions. The data structure contains one record per

field with the type of each record based on the type of the field: a bit-sized, integer field results in a long integer record, and a byte-sized, data field results in a unsigned character pointer record.

2. A function allowing an action to recognize and parse a message when it is received. The message reader function converts integer fields from network byte order to host byte order, checks that constant fields have an appropriate value, and assigns to each character pointer record the matching location in the incoming message. The reader function returns true if the message being parsed is recognized, according to its size and the value of constant fields, and false otherwise.

3. A function enabling an action to store the message an a buffer for transmission. The message writer function converts integer records to network byte order and copies their value as well as the data pointed to by character pointer records to a temporary buffer for transmission.

The message definition notation is intended primarily to support the message formats used by common Internet protocols, specifically the "box" diagrams common in IETF RFCs. Neither the message definition notation of TAP nor the code generated is intended to handle every possible format for messages. For messages which cannot be handled in TAP, the message definition can be declared "external" in the TAP source. In this case, the two functions are not generated and must be provided by the programmer. By hand-generating the two functions, messages that do not match the formats of the notation can be accommodated.

TAP processes

A TAP process is also represented in the C code by three components:

1. A pair of data structures, called the *state data structure* and the *tag data structure,* with the state data structure containing the process's state and the tag data structure containing information describing the process;

2. A pair of initialization functions, the first setting up the state data structure and the second setting up the tag data structure of the process; and

3. A set of action functions, with one function per action in the process;

Process data structures.   The state data structure contains records for each of the process's constants and variables. The fields are referenced by the code of the process's actions. Fields in the structure are either unsigned integers, abstract addresses, or arrays of one of those basic types.

The tag data structure has a generic prefix common to all processes, allowing the protocol runtime system to interact with the process. The tag data structure contains records holding:

- A text string naming the process,

- A reference to the state data structure for the process,

- Lists of action function records for actions with local and receive guards,

- A list of time variables used by timeout guards in the process, along with the function implementing the action, and

- A buffer for messages sent locally between processes executing within the same runtime system,

Process initialization.   Each process uses two initialization functions, one for each of the two data structures. The first sets the records of the state data structure with the initial value of the process's variables and constants.

The second function sets up the tag data structure, including calling the function to initialize the state data structure, setting up the local message buffer and the records for the process's action functions and time variables. Additionally, this function prepares the information needed to assign values to abstract addresses which are part of the process's state. Finally, this function informs the APC runtime system about the process.

As described previously, there is no way to specify a value for an address variable or constant from within TAP, and the address variables and constants are translated into state data structure records containing abstract addresses. One way that a variable address acquires a value is when used in a receive guard—the process of recognizing the message sets the variable to the address of the message's sender. On the other hand, it is necessary to identify a remote process in order to begin to communicate with it. Many address variables or constants need to be initially assigned an address, either for the base network protocol or for local communication. As part of the process structure initialization, the generated code registers with the runtime system the identifier used by the process for each of its addresses as a text string. This identifier is associated with the location of the address constant or variable in the process's state. Since the variables and constants can be arrays, the identifier is additionally associated with the dimensions of the variable or constant—a non-array simply has zero dimensions. This registration is used to identify the address when it is assigned a value by external code, using functions provided by the APC runtime system described on page 78.

Action functions.   The actions of a process are translated to C functions. The parameters of the functions depend on the type of the action guard, although all action functions take the tag data structure of the process containing the action as a parameter. Actions with local and timeout guards produce functions with no other arguments while actions with receive guards produce functions that also take a buffer containing the received message, the message's size, and the abstract address of the sender.

For local and receive guards, the action functions logically take the form of a single C **if** statement. The translated guard of the action makes up the condition of the statement, with local guards having a translated predicate, and receive guards calling message parsing functions. The translated statements of the action become the body of the if statement. Timeout guards do not have any predicate associated with the guard and therefore the functions for such actions do not have the overall conditional structure, but simply contain the translated statements.

The integer returned value of the action function is used by the runtime system to distinguish three possibilities:

- A returned value of zero indicates that the guard of the action was false. In this case, the statements of the action function have not executed and the state of the process has not changed.

- A returned value greater than zero indicates that the guard of the action was true. In this case, the statements of the action function have executed and the state of the process may have been changed.

- A returned value less than zero indicates that an unexpected error has occurred. Such errors will terminate the runtime system.

The generated code is linked with a runtime system to produce the executable protocol. The information provided by the compiler is used by the runtime system to implement TAP's concrete execution model.

APC runtime interfaces

Like yacc, the Austin Protocol Compiler generates a protocol implementation that is invoked from an external program and that in turn invokes other external functions. The interfaces between the external program and the protocol implementation, and between the protocol implementation and external functions are described by C functions and data structures. The next section describes the interface between the external program and the protocol implementation, and the following section describes the interface to code called from TAP statements. Finally, the last section in this chapter describes the interface between the runtime system and the functions recognizing incoming messages and and buffering outgoing messages, as used by messages which are declared "external."

Initializing and executing the runtime system

Preparing to execute a TAP process is essentially a four step procedure:

1. The first step is to initialize the protocol engine, described on page 80, and the base network protocol. The function used to do this with the UDP base network protocol is:

    UDP_initialize_engine(int port)

    This function accepts a UDP port number on which to listen for incoming messages.

2. The second step is to initialize each process that will execute within the protocol engine, using a function generated by the compiler:

$$\text{process\_}p(\text{char *process\_name,}$$
$$p\text{\_state\_t *state,}$$
$$p\text{\_process\_t *process)}$$

The **p** will be replaced by the name of the TAP process. The process_name argument provides a text identifier for the local message-passing address of the process, allowing more than one instance of a TAP process to be executed within a single protocol engine while allowing another process to send messages locally to this instance. The state and tag data structure definitionss are generated by the compiler, but instances of each must be allocated by the code calling this function; the handling of these two arguments is described on 75.

3. Since there is no way to initialize an address variable or constant in TAP, the code invoking the protocol engine must do it, calling the following function for each address variable or constant:

$$\textbf{APC\_set\_address(APC\_process\_t process,}$$
$$\textbf{char *identifier,}$$
$$\textbf{APC\_address\_type\_t type,}$$
$$\textbf{char *address)}$$

The process and the identifier arguments identify the address variable or constant to be initialized; the identifier is the name of the address variable or constant in the TAP process definition. If the actual address is an element of an array, the identifier argument should also have an array reference suffix describing the particular element to be initialized: "addr[1]", for example. The type argument indicates whether the address is either:

- A base network protocol address, in which case the address argument should be a string describing the address according to the convention of the base network protocol interface. For UDP, this is "hostname:port number", the remote host name or IP address followed by the remote UDP port number separated by a colon, or

- A local address, in which case the address argument should match the process_name of a local process, given in the process initialization function.

4. The final step is to execute the protocol engine:

APC_engine()

This function does not terminate unless the protocol engine reports an error.

All of these functions may report errors via their returned values.

Invoking C functions from TAP

Because the protocol implementation generated by APC is embedded in C, functions invoked by the protocol process's statements are called as normal C functions, with the following argument conventions:

- Integer values are passed as C long integers, and

- Data values, such as fields in messages, are passed as unsigned character pointers.

Values may be passed as arguments to functions or may be returned by functions, as described in the grammar on page 28.

Message functions

As described previously on page 74, messages may be declared to be external, in which case the programmer must provide implementations of the functions reading a newly received message and writing an outgoing message to a buffer. The prototypes of these two functions, with m replaced by the name of the message, are:

- read_m(unsigned char *incoming, int in_length, m *dest)

- write_m(m *src, unsigned char *outgoing, int out_length)

The dest and src arguments are pointers to the data structure describing the message's fields; this structure is always generated by the compiler and the type of the structure is named after the message. The incoming, in_length, outgoing, and out_length parameters describe the buffer containing the incoming message or to which the outgoing message should be written.

Architecture of the runtime system

The runtime system is divided into three components:

- The abstract protocol engine and interface made up of approximately 1000 lines of C.

- The base network protocol interface, including sending and receiving messages and managing address values. For the current version, the base network protocol is limited to UDP and is made up of approximately 350 lines of C.

- The local message passing interface, interacting with TAP processes in the same way as the base network protocol although only transferring messages between processes executing in the same runtime engine. This interface is made up of approximately 250 lines of C.

The core of the runtime system is the protocol engine, illustrated in Figure 6. During the engine's execution, it maintains the engine maintains references to:

- The processes that are running within the engine,

- All of the local and receive action records, with pointers to the functions implementing the actions and to the process containing each action, and

- All of the time variables associated with each timeout-guarded action in the processes running in the engine.

The protocol engine supports the execution of multiple local processes by maintaining the references to the action records without regard to the process containing the actions or time variables. For example, if multiple processes are running within a single engine, when a base network protocol message is received the receive action functions from all processes running in the engine are allowed to try to parse it. The first action function which recognizes the message executes the statements from its action, with the state for the process supplied from the action record. After a message has been recognized and handled, no further receive action functions are tried with the message.

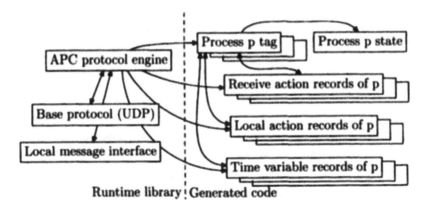

Figure 6.3: APC runtime architecture. Each process has pointers to its state structure and to its own action records. The protocol engine has pointers to each process and to lists of all of the action records.

Implementation of the concrete execution model

The protocol engine described previously is designed to ensure the guarantees of the TAP concrete execution model. The algorithm used by the engine is shown in Figure 6.4. This algorithm ensures the following conditions of protocol execution that satisfy the concrete execution model from page 42:

1. The execution of the engine proceeds by invoking the functions implementing the actions of each process serially. Each of the functions executes atomically with respect to the other actions of the process containing it, ensuring that no two actions from the same process are executed concurrently.

2. The action choice event of the concrete execution model is performed by the protocol engine in steps 1,2,5, and 6, outside of the execution of any action function. As a result, no action function can be executing when another action is chosen for execution.

3. The compiler generates each action function to correctly implement the statements of the body of the action, ensuring the proper execution of each action.

1. Attempt to execute each local action function once.

2. If any process has messages waiting in its local buffer, attempt to execute the process's receive actions with each waiting message.

3. Calculate a new delay value:

   (a) If any local or receive action function executed in step 1 or 2, the new delay is zero;

   (b) If there are outstanding time variables, the delay is the time until the next time variable expires;

   (c) Otherwise, the delay is unbounded, and the process will wait until a message arrives from the base network protocol.

4. Wait for the delay to expire, if there is one, or for a message to be received from the base network protocol.

5. If a message has been received, attempt to execute each process's receive action functions with the waiting message.

6. If the time variable delay has expired, execute the corresponding timeout action function.

7. Return to step 1.

Figure 6.4: Algorithm of the APC protocol engine.

4. Because message transmission is decoupled from the execution of each action function, by the base network protocol and by the local message interface, no two operations on the same message can be simultaneous.

5. Each action function is assumed to execute quickly, relative to the duration of the timeout delay. As a result, the passage of time can be assumed to occur in step 4, outside the execution of any action.

The assumptions concerning message delay and errors described on pages 45 and 45 are based on the behavior of the base network protocol. The UDP base protocol satisfies these conditions, and while the local message transmission mechanism does not delay messages and should not suffer from faults in the same way as the base network protocol, its behavior does not contradict the assumptions.

The concrete model's timeout behavior described on page 46 is likewise based on the behavior of implemented protocol actions—each action function is assumed to execute quickly, relative to the duration of the timeout delay. As a result, the passage of time is assumed to occur entirely in step 4, and the choice of executing an action with a timeout guard can be assumed to occur in step 6.

Finally, the overall algorithm of Figure 6.4 enforces the local fairness conditions described on page 46—no action in a process can be prevented from executing indefinitely by the execution of other actions, since every action function is invoked before any one is invoked again.

The algorithm of Figure 6.4 is also the source of the requirement for protocol quiescence on page 19: if any local action becomes enabled, then it must be executed or disabled before the process will wait again. The algorithm makes it impossible for any process to wait when a local action is enabled.

The Austin Protocol Compiler and its runtime system implement the guarantees made by the concrete execution model, and the concrete execution model is equivalent to the abstract execution model. As a result, the behavior of an implemented protocol will be the same as the behavior expected from the protocol in the abstract model.

This page intentionally left blank

Chapter 7

TWO EXAMPLES

In order to validate the Austin Protocol Compiler, we took two protocols described elsewhere, re-specified them in TAP, and completed the framework needed to create prototype implementations of them. These two protocols serve as both a sanity check on the behavior of an implementation produced by APC and as functional examples of relatively complex protocols built using APC.

The first protocol is the secret exchange protocol, which is intended to securely change message integrity keys used between two network routers. This protocol is the simpler of the two examples in this chapter and demonstrates the basic functionality of APC. After describing the background of the secret exchange protocol and presenting its TAP specification as well as the outside code needed by it, two traces of its execution are presented, the first showing the protocol executing normally and the second showing the behavior of the protocol reacting to an attacking adversary.

The second protocol is the accelerated heartbeat protocol, which is used to monitor the status of the processes involved in the protocol as well as the network between the processes. This protocol is more complex since it dynamically adjusts its timeout delays in response to message losses. After describing its background and presenting its specification and code, three traces are presented, showing the protocol's normal behavior, its response to a permanently failed process, and its response to a temporary series of lost messages.

The secret exchange protocol

Current TCP/IP networks are vulnerable to a number of security problems. One class of security problems that is particularly difficult to handle is called a denial-of-service attack, whose aim is to exhaust the resources of a network or of a host, so that normal services provided by the network or the host are reduced or denied. Two examples of denial-of-service attacks are:

- "Smurf" attacks[51], which use the ICMP Echo Request/Reply messages[52] to attack a network host *d*. The attacker inserts an Echo Request into the network with the source address forged to be the address of *d* and with a destination address set to a multicast address for every host on the network. Every host on the network receiving such a request sends an Echo Reply message to *d*, flooding the network and *d*.[1]

- SYN attacks[53], which attack the TCP connection protocol of a network host *d*. Normally, a TCP connection is opened by a three-way handshake: a host *c* sending *d* a message with the SYN flag set, after which *d* replies to *c* with a message having the SYN and ACK flags set, and *c* completing the handshake with a message having an ACK flag set; following the handshake, both hosts know that the connection has been successfully created. When *d* receives the SYN message, it must reserve resources for the new connection, and these resources are the target of the attack; if many SYN messages are received in a short time, *d* will run out of resources and be unable to open new connections until those half-connections time out. In order to make the attack harder to defend against, the attacker forges the source addresses of the SYN messages, setting each to the address of a different host.

Denial-of-service attacks are difficult to defend against because there needs to be no relationship between the attacker and the contents of the forged messages constituting the attack. Other attacks, however, are possible using similar techniques. In general, an attacker can insert forged messages, modify existing messages, and replay old messages as part of an attack.

Hop integrity

In order to defend against these kinds of attacks, we introduced protocols to provide *hop integrity*[54] for a network. A network provides hop integrity iff:

---

[1]Hosts should not respond to ICMP messages sent to multicast addresses, but historically this condition has not always been implemented correctly.

1. Whenever a router p receives a message m supposedly from an adjacent router q, then p can determine whether m was modified by an attacker after it was sent by q and before it was received by p.

2. Whenever p receives m supposedly from q, then p can determine whether m is a copy of an earlier message received by p.

Hop integrity can be provided by two protocols for transferring data messages between two routers: the weak integrity protocol and the strong integrity protocol. The weak integrity protocol adds to each message a message digest computed of the text of the message and a secret key shared between the two routers, satisfying the first requirement of hop integrity. The strong integrity protocol also adds sequence numbers (using "soft" state) to prevent message replay and satisfy the second requirement of hop integrity.

An attacker attempting to modify a message between q and p will be detected by the weak integrity protocol. An attacker attempting to replay a message between q and p will be detected by the strong integrity protocol. Finally, an attack made up of forged messages will also be detected, since

- If a forged message appears to have traveled through q, it will not contain the correct message digest, and

- If forged messages appear to have come from a host on the subnetwork between q and p, traditional ingress filtering[55] will detect the forgery.

Implementation of the secret exchange protocol

Both the weak integrity protocol and the strong integrity protocol make use of a secret key shared between the two routers executing the processes of the protocols. By design, the secret key should be changed often. Generating and exchanging the secret key is the function of the secret exchange protocol. One process of the secret exchange protocol, pe, is executed by the router p and is shown in Figure 7.1, Figure 7.2 and Figure 7.3. The other process, qe, is executed by q and is defined symmetrically. Figure 7.4 defines the two messages used by the secret exchange protocol.

The messages used by the protocol are a key change request and a key change reply:

```
process pe
   const  Rp : integer = 0;
          Bq : integer = 0;
          te : integer = 20000;
          tr : integer = 1000;
          qe : address
   var  sp : integer = 0;
        sq : array [2] of integer = 0;
        d, e : integer;
        initialize : boolean = true
   . . .
```

Figure 7.1: The secret exchange protocol, part 1.

- The rqst message contains a one byte field for the message type and an 8 byte data field containing two 32 bit keys. The first key in the field is the current key used for sending messages to *p*, and the second is the newly generated key.

- The rply message contains a one byte type field and a single 32 bit data field acknowledging the new key.

Process pe uses the following constants and variables:

- The constant Rp is the long-term private key of pe and the constant Bq is the long-term public key of qe. The long-term keys of each process are inputs to the protocol, and should be set by the network administrator. In the prototype described here, the values are arbitrary.

- The constant te is the interval between secret key changes. This interval should be relatively short, on the order of a few minutes. The constant tr is the timeout for retransmitting key change requests. This timeout should be an upper bound on the round-trip delay between the two routers, on the order of a few seconds.

- The constant qe is the address of the process qe.

- The variable sp is the secret key currently used when sending messages to qe.

```
...
begin
  initialize → act sendrqst in 0; initialize := false
| timeout sendrqst → sq[1] := NEWSCR();
                     rqst.e := NCR(Bq, 2, sq[0], sq[1]);
                     send rqst to qe;
                     log("sent rqst (%d, %d)", sq[0], sq[1]);
                     act resend in tr;
                     act sendrqst in te
| rcv rqst from qe → d, e := DCR(Bq, 0, rqst.e), DCR(Bq, 1, rqst.e);
                     log("received rqst (%d, %d)", d, e);
                     if (sp = d) ∨ (sp = e) → sp := e;
                                              reply.e := NCR(Bq, 1, sp);
                                              send reply to qe;
                                              log("sent reply (%d)", sp);
                     | (sp ≠ d) ∧ (sp ≠ e) → log("detect adversary: bad rqst")
                     fi
...
```

Figure 7.2: The secret exchange protocol, part 2.

- The variable sq is an array containing the old and new secret keys used when receiving messages from qe.

- The variables d and e are two temporary values.

- The variable initialize is a flag used to enable the action initializing the process. This action, the first in process pe, is executed once when the process begins and sets in motion the first key change.

Finally, pe uses the following C functions for encryption, decryption, and generating keys. Since the implementation discussed here is a prototype, simple encryption algorithms are used. These algorithms are not strong enough for production use.

- NEWSCR generates and returns a new secret key. NEWSCR uses the rand() C library function; a production implementation should use a more secure random number generator.

unsigned long NEWSCR(void)

. . .

```
| rcv reply from qe → d := DCR(Rp, 0, reply.e);
                      log("received reply (%d)", d);
                      if sq[1] = d → sq[0] := sq[1]
                      | sq[1] ≠ d → log("detect adversary: bad rply")
                      fi
| timeout resend → if sq[0] ≠ sq[1] → rqst.e := NCR(Bq, 2, sq[0], sq[1]);
                                      send rqst to qe;
                                      log("resent rqst (%d, %d)", sq[0], sq[1]);
                                      act resend in tr
                   | sq[0] = sq[1] → skip
                   fi
end
```

Figure 7.3: The secret exchange protocol, part 3.

```
message rqst                        message reply
begin                               begin
   type : 8 bits = 1,                  type : 8 bits = 2,
   e : 8 bytes                         e : 4 bytes
end                                 end
```

Figure 7.4: Messages from the secret exchange protocol.

- NCR accepts at least two arguments, and encrypts the subsequent count unsigned long arguments with key, returning the resulting buffer. NCR uses simple XOR encryption; a production implementation should use a much stronger algorithm.

```
char *NCR(unsigned long key, unsigned long count, ...)
```

- DCR decrypts the unsigned long value at offset of buffer using key. Like NCR, DCR uses XOR encryption.

```
unsigned long DCR(unsigned long key,
                  unsigned long offset,
                  char *buffer)
```

- Finally, log announces important messages; the current version prints the message to the process' standard output. Other options include logging the message remotely, using syslog, for example.

void log(char *message)

These C functions are implemented in two separate modules each made up of a source file and a header file. The TAP file containing the definition of pe has include directives which bring the header files into the generated C code for the process.

For pe to change its secret sq, four steps need to be performed. Each of these four steps is represented by an action in pe and qe:

1. First, pe generates a new key, sq[1], and encrypts the concatenation of the old key, sq[0], and the new key using qe's long-term public key, Bq. The resulting request message is sent to qe. This step is handled by the sendrqst timeout action in Figure 7.2.

2. Second, when qe receives the request message, it decrypts the contents using its long-term private key, Rq, and obtains the old key and new key. Then qe checks that its current sq equals the old key from the request message, installs the new key as its current key, and sends a reply message containing the encryption of the new key using pe's long-term public key Bp. This step is handled by the action guarded by "**rcv** rqst" in Figure 7.2.

3. Third, pe waits until it receives a reply message from qe containing the new key encrypted using Bp. This indicates that qe has accepted the new key. This step is handled by the action guarded by "**rcv** rply" in Figure 7.3.

4. If pe sends the request to qe but does not receive a reply for tr milliseconds, the request message or the reply message has been lost. In this case, pe resends the request message to qe. This step is handled by the resend timeout in Figure 7.3.

At all times, the secret key used for the integrity protocol message digest for messages sent from *p* to *q* is sp. The secret key used for messages sent from

```
pe_state_t state;
pe_process_t process;

log("start");
UDP_initialize_engine(atoi(argv[1]));
process_pe("pe", &state, &process);
APC_set_address((APC_process_t) &process,
                "qe",
                APC_lowlevel_address,
                argv[2]);
APC_engine();
```

Figure 7.5: C statements executing process pe. The program in this example accepts two command line arguments. The first, argv[1], is the numeric UDP port number on which process pe should listen for messages. The second, argv[2], is the address of process qe, including the hostname and port number.

q to p is either sq[0] or sq[1]; sq[0] is normally used, but if the keys are in the process of being changed, sq[1] may be necessary. The two integrity protocols try the two keys in that order.

The definition for pe along with the definition of the rqst and rply messages and the include directives for the C functions described previously make up the source code of the protocol itself. Given the TAP source, the Austin Protocol Compiler generates a C module, made up of a source file and a header file, containing the translated code and data structures for the protocol. This module is then combined with a program skeleton to create the executable implementation.

Figure 7 presents the program skeleton, the code used to set up and execute pe from the C main() function. The first argument to the program, argv[1], is the UDP port number on which pe should listen for incoming messages and the second argument, argv[2], has the hostname and UDP port number of qe.

Since the reliability of the secret exchange protocol is paramount, it has been verified[54], and the code generated by the compiler was compared with the specification. As seen in Chapter 6, the Austin Protocol Compiler maintains the guarantees necessary for the correctness of the protocol. As a result, the execution of the protocol matches the expected behavior of the specification, avoiding the intrinsic problems of network protocol development.

Behavior of the secret exchange protocol

```
apcc pe.ap
gcc -IAPC-runtime-directory -I../common^a -g -O2 pe-main.c
gcc -IAPC-runtime-directory -I../common -g -O2 sep.c^b
gcc -IAPC-runtime-directory -I../common -g -O2 pe.c
gcc -g -O2 -o key-exchange pe-main.o sep.o pe.o \
    -LAPC-runtime-directory -IAPC^c ../common/libcommon.a
```

---
^a The common library contains the log function.
^b The sep module contains the encryption functions.
^c The APC library contains the runtime engine.

Figure 7.6: Compiling the key exchange process.

The C code for the process described in Figure 7.1, Figure 7.2, Figure 7.3 and the messages in Figure 7.4 was generated and linked with a main() function described in Figure 7 and the logging and encryption functions described previously as well as the APC runtime library. The sequence of commands performing these steps is shown in Figure 7.6. The result was an executable file called key-exchange, which was used to create the execution traces in Figure 7.7 and Figure 7.8. In both traces, key-exchange was executed twice, as processes pe and qe. Both processes executed on the same machine, to ensure that the trace timestamps remained correct.

Figure 7.7 shows the beginning of an execution trace of the normal behavior of the secret exchange protocol. Each line in the trace represents a single line of output produced by the log function, with a timestamp of the event at the left. Each request includes the old and new secrets, and each reply identifies the new secrets being acknowledged.

Notice that requests to change secrets are generated approximately 20 seconds after the last secret change, and that message retransmissions are sent after approximately 1 second. Both of these delays are specified in Figure 7.1, by the constant values of 20000 for te and 1000 for tr. The two constants are used in activation statements in Figure 7.2 and Figure 7.3.

	Log messages	
Seconds	**pe**	**qe**
0.000000		start
0.000327		send rqst (0, 57606676)
1.001112		resend rqst (0, 57606676)[a]
1.259442	start	
1.259777		recv rqst (0, 1899027511)[b]
1.259803		send reply (1899027511)
1.259838	send rqst (0, 1899027511)	
1.259872	recv reply (1899027511)	
2.001939		resend rqst (0, 57606676)
2.002043	recv rqst (0, 57606676)	
2.002067	send reply (57606676)	
2.002122		recv reply (57606676)
20.001195		send rqst (57606676, 1126385251)[c]
20.001308	recv rqst (57606676, 1126385251)	
20.001334	send reply (1126385251)	
20.001377		recv reply (1126385251)
21.260038		recv rqst (1899027511, 2004821925)
21.260101		send reply (2004821925)
21.260136	send rqst (1899027511, 2004821925)	
21.260173	recv reply (2004821925)	

[a]Process qe sent its first request before pe was started.
[b]This request matches the trace entry by pe at 1.259838 seconds; it appears a context switch occurred between sending the message and calling the log function. Misordered entries such as this appear several times in this example.
[c]This entry begins the first periodic key change.

Figure 7.7: Normal execution trace of the key exchange protocol.

Figure 7.8 shows a partial execution trace of pe under attack. The process labelled "attacker" simulates an attacking host located between q and p. This attacking host does not know the long-term keys used between q and p and is attempting to forge secret change requests and replies. In the two attacks shown, the forgery was detected because the decrypted secrets did not match what process pe was expecting.

While the correctness of the secret exchange protocol has been verified and the implementation described here appears to function correctly, further work is necessary. For example, experimentation with the implementation is needed for the following extrinsic aspects of the secret exchange protocol:

	Log messages	
Seconds	**attacker**	**pe**
0.000000		start
. . .		
1.054219	start	
. . .		
11.055430	send rqst attack (787824220, 2092571940)[a]	
11.055562		recv rqst (1384642625, 13163321)[b]
11.055588		detect adversary: bad rqst[c]
. . .		
21.055868	send rply attack (1194734761)	
21.056046		recv reply (1040998259)
21.056072		detect adversary: bad rply[d]

[a]This rqst contains the current key used by the integrity protocol between *q* and *p*, as a worst-case scenario, and new, randomly generated key known by the attacker. It is not encrypted with the long-term keys known to pe and qe.

[b]Since the wrong long-term key was used to encrypt the rqst, the decrypted current key does not match what pe expects.

[c]The attacker has been detected.

[d]As above, since the wrong key was used to encrypt the forged rply, it does not match what pe expects and the attacker is detected.

Figure 7.8: Execution trace of the key exchange protocol under attack.

- The proper values for the timeout delays, te and tr, of the protocol.

- The appropriate sizes for the encryption keys used by the protocol and the appropriate encryption algorithms to use for NCR, DCR, and NEWSCR.

These parameters depend on the security of the encryption algorithms as well as their performance, particularly the message digest algorithm used by the integrity protocols. The prototype of the secret exchange protocol created with the Austin Protocol Compiler is a first step for these experiments.

The accelerated heartbeat protocol

A fundamental construct for tolerating faults in computer networks is a heartbeat protocol. A heartbeat protocol allows processes in a network to periodically exchange beat messages. As long as a process p keeps receiving beat messages from a process q, p recognizes that q and the communication medium from q to p are both up. If p does not receive any beat messages from q for a long time, p recognizes that q has terminated or failed or that the communication medium from q to p has failed. In this case, p itself terminates. Therefore, a heartbeat protocol ensures that if one or more processes in a program fail or terminate, then every other process in the program terminates.

There are three contradictory objectives for a heartbeat protocol:

1. In order to reduce the overhead of the protocol, as few beat messages as possible should be sent.

2. In order to increase protocol responsiveness, the detection delay (which is the longest period that can pass after one process terminates and before the heartbeat protocol causes all processes to terminate) should be small.

3. In order to improve reliability, the probability of premature termination (which is the probability that the heartbeat protocol causes all processes to terminate due to the loss of beat messages and not due to the termination of a process or the permanent failure of the network) should be small.

It is possible to make a compromise between the objectives and construct a heartbeat protocol which is configurable for different requirements and network conditions. This protocol is called the accelerated heartbeat protocol[56]. It minimizes the protocol overhead while providing an acceptable tradeoff between detection delay and the probability of premature termination.

Consider the case where the network that has only two processes, $p[0]$ and $p[1]$. The communication between $p[0]$ and $p[1]$ can be partitioned into successive time periods. In each period, $p[0]$ sends a beat message to $p[1]$ then waits to receive back a beat message from $p[1]$. The length of each period depends on the events that occurred in the preceding period according to the following three rules:

1. If in a period, $p[0]$ sends a beat message to $p[1]$ and receives a beat message from $p[1]$, then $p[0]$ makes the length of the next period a large value *tmax* (irrespective of the length of the current period). The value of *tmax* is determined by the acceptable detection delay and by the probability of premature termination.

2. If in a period, $p[0]$ sends a beat message to $p[1]$ but does not receive a beat message from $p[1]$, then $p[0]$ makes the length of the next period half that of the current period.

3. If the length of the next period ever becomes less than *tmin*, an upper bound on the round trip delay for beat messages between $p[0]$ and $p[1]$, then $p[0]$ terminates and stops sending beat messages to $p[1]$.

Rule 1 is adopted to ensure that when $p[0]$ and $p[1]$ and the communication medium between them are all up (a typical situation), the rate of sending beat messages is kept small. Rules 2 and 3 are adopted so that when $p[0]$ suspects a failure or termination, $p[0]$ tries to refute this suspicion several times in a short span before it finally accepts its suspicion and terminates. Thus, these two rules ensure that both the detection delay and the probability of premature termination are kept small.

From these three rules, if $p[0]$ does not receive any beat message for a period of $2tmax$, then $p[0]$ terminates. Moreover, if $p[1]$ does not receive any beat message for a period of $3tmax - tmin$ (and so it does not send any beat messages for the same period), then $p[1]$ recognizes that $p[0]$ has already terminated and $p[1]$ itself terminates.

To understand the period $3tmax - tmin$, consider the following scenario:

1. $p[0]$ sends and receives beat messages. The period is *tmax*.

2. The network fails; all further messages are lost.

3. After a period of *tmax*, $p[0]$ sends a beat message.

4. After another period of *tmax*, $p[0]$ has received no beat message. It sends a beat message and makes the next period *tmax*/2.

5. $p[0]$ continues to halve the period until it terminates.

The time between steps 1 and 3 is *tmax*, between steps 3 and 4 is *tmax*, and between steps 4 and 5 is bounded by $tmax - tmin$. Thus, the period between steps 1 and 5 is bounded by $3tmax - tmin$.

The two-process heartbeat protocol can be extended to a protocol that involves $n + 1$ processes, $p[0]$ to $p[n]$. In this extended version of the accelerated heartbeat protocol, $p[0]$ executes a acts as $p[0]$ above, except that it communicates with every other process. The communication between $p[0]$ and the processes $p[i]$, $1 \leq i \leq n$, can be partitioned into periods. In each period, process $p[0]$ sends a beat message to every $p[i]$ process and then waits to receive a beat message from every $p[i]$ process. When $p[0]$ receives a beat message from any $p[i]$, $p[0]$ records this fact.

At the end of each period, process $p[0]$ computes the length of the next period as follows: First, $p[0]$ computes the length of the next period for each process $p[i]$ as described previously. Second, $p[0]$ selects the smallest delay to be the length of the next period.

The analysis of how values for the acceptable detection delay, the probability that a beat message will be lost by a single error, and the upper bound on the round trip delay combine to set the values of *tmax* and the probability of premature termination is described elsewhere[56] for both the two process and n process accelerated heartbeat protocol. The remainder of this section discusses the implementation of a three-process accelerated heartbeat protocol.

Implementation of the accelerated heartbeat protocol

```
message beat
begin
   type : 8 bits = 1,
   id : 8 bits
end
```

Figure 7.9: Message definition for the accelerated heartbeat protocol.

The beat message exchanged by the processes of the accelerated heartbeat protocol is defined in Figure 7.9. In this message, the type field indicates a beat message and the id field provides a number identifying the $p[1]$ and $p[2]$ to $p[0]$.

The first process definition in the protocol, p0, is the "root" process. The definition of p0 is shown in Figure 7.10 and Figure 7.11. The second process definition, pn, is executed twice, as the child processes $p[1]$ and $p[2]$. The definition of pn is shown in Figure 7.12.

```
process p0
const tmin : integer = 1000;
      tmax : integer = 10000;
      pn : array [2] of address
var rcvd : array [2] of boolean = true;
    tm : array [2] of integer;
    t : integer = 10000;
    k : 0..2;
    p : address;
    initialize : boolean = true
begin
  initialize → k := 0;
                do k < 2 → tm[k], beat.id := tmax, k;
                          send beat to pn[k]; k := k + 1
                od;
                act tick in t;
                initialize := false
...
```

*Figure 7.10: The accelerated heartbeat protocol, process **p**[0], part 1.*

The definition of p0 in Figure 7.10 uses the following constants and variables:

- The constant tmin is an upper bound on the round trip delay between the
  process in the protocol, to be used as a lower bound on the timeout delay
  for the heartbeat period. For this prototype implementation, this constant
  is set to 1 second.

- The constant tmax is the normal period for sending beat messages. The
  detection delay for failures is $3tmax$. For this implementation, it is set to
  10 seconds.

- The constant pn is an array containing the addresses of the child processes. Since this array is constant, the values of these addresses must be
  set by the program using APC_set_address before executing the protocol
  engine.

- The variable rcvd is an array of boolean values indicating whether a beat
  message has been received from the corresponding child process in the
  current round.

...

```
| timeout tick → log("tick");
              k := 0;
              do k < 2 → if rcvd[k] → tm[k] := tmax
                         | ¬rcvd[k] → tm[k] := tm[k] / 2
                         fi; k := k + 1
              od;
              if tm[0] <= tm[1] → t := tm[0]
              | tm[0] > tm[1] → t := tm[1]
              fi;
              if t < tmin → log("exit");
                            exit(2)
              | t ≥ tmin → k := 0;
                           do k < 2 → beat.id, rcvd[k] := k, false;
                                      send beat to pn[k]; k := k + 1
                           od
              fi;
              act tick in t
| rcv beat from p → log("rcv beat(%d)", beat.id);
                    rcvd[beat.id] := true
end
```

Figure 7.11: The accelerated heartbeat protocol, process $p[0]$, part 2.

- The variable tm is an array containing the heartbeat period for the protocol between $p[0]$ and the corresponding child process.

- The variable t is The minimum value from tm, to be used as the delay for the next round. Initially, t is set to tmax.

- The variables k and p are two temporary variables; k is used as an index into the various arrays and p is used when receiving messages from a child process.

- The variable initialize guards the first action of the process; it is initially true but set to false after the first action is executed.

The first action of p0 in Figure 7.10, sends an initial beat message to the children and sets up the delay for the first round. Each beat message contains an id field which identifies the child process to which the message is sent.

```
process pn
const tmin : integer = 1000;
      tmax : integer = 10000;
      p0 : address
var initialize : boolean = true
begin
   initialize → act inactive in 3*tmax - tmin;
                     initialize := false
 | rcv beat from p0 → log("rcv beat(%d)", beat.id);
                     send beat to p0;
                     act inactive in 3*tmax - tmin
 | timeout inactive → log("exit");
                     exit (2)
end
```

Figure 7.12: The accelerated heartbeat protocol, process $p[1]$ *and* $p[2]$.

The second action of p0 in Figure 7.11 computes the delay for the next round according to the rules from page 96 and whether or not a beat message has been received in the current round from each child. This action potentially either:

- Terminates the program, if $t <$ tmin, or

- Sends a new round of beat messages and activates the timeout for the next round, if $t \geq$ **tmin**.

The third action of p0 in Figure 7.11 simply receives a beat message from a child and marks the element of the rcvd array based on the id field in the message.

The definition of pn in Figure 7.12 uses only a single initialize variable, to enable the initial action which sets the initial delay after which pn will execute the third action. The second action of pn receives the beat message from p0, returns it, and resets the delay for the third action. The third action, enabled only when pn has not received a beat message in the $3tmax - tmin$ time period, terminates the process.

Behavior of the accelerated heartbeat protocol

The TAP processes described in Figure 7.10, Figure 7.11 and Figure 7.12 and the message in Figure 7.9 were compiled and linked with driver programs, the APC runtime library, and the logging function. The processes of the protocol were executed on the same machine, in order to generate an accurate trace of the activities of the processes. The behavior of the protocol when executed normally is demonstrated in the trace in Figure 7.13. In this trace, beat messages are exchanged every *tmax* milliseconds.

	Log messages		
Seconds	*p*[0]	*p*[1]	*p*[2]
0.000000		start	
0.961388			start
2.240651	start		
2.241132		rcv beat(0)	
2.241243			rcv beat(1)
2.241308	rcv beat(0)		
2.241334	rcv beat(1)		
12.242256	tick		
12.242458		rcv beat(0)	
12.242529			rcv beat(1)
12.242581	rcv beat(0)		
12.242602	rcv beat(1)		
22.242736	tick		
22.242927		rcv beat(0)	
22.242997			rcv beat(1)
22.243049	rcv beat(0)		
22.243070	rcv beat(1)		

Figure 7.13: Normal execution trace of 3-process accelerated heartbeat protocol.

More complex behavior from the accelerated heartbeat protocol is shown in Figure 7.14. In this trace, *p*[1] was terminated after a few seconds of execution and then restarted, allowing the heartbeat protocol to recover. Process *p*[1] was down for approximately 13 seconds, missing two rounds.

Finally, Figure 7.15 shows the behavior of the accelerated heartbeat protocol when *p*[1] permanently fails after a few seconds of execution. As designed, *p*[0] terminates within 3*tmax* milliseconds or 30 seconds, and *p*[2] terminates within a further 3*tmax* milliseconds after the final beat message is sent.

One use of the accelerated heartbeat protocol is in monitoring existing protocols which do not have flexible heartbeat mechanisms, as described in Gouda and McGuire[57]. The system described in that paper uses a hand-coded version of the accelerated heartbeat to monitor traffic over a TCP connection with a minimal impact on the protocol using the TCP connection. An earlier TAP specification of the accelerated heartbeat was integral in developing the hand-coded implementation.

Seconds	Log messages p[0]	p[1]	p[2]
0.000000		start	
1.766863			start
2.564945	start		
2.565327			rcv beat(1)
2.565401	rcv beat(1)		
2.565553		rcv beat(0)	
2.565611	rcv beat(0)		
9.797133		terminate[a]	
12.565980	tick		
12.566285			rcv beat(1)
12.566341	rcv beat(1)		
22.566407	tick[b]		
22.566636			rcv beat(1)
22.566696	rcv beat(1)		
22.847763		start[c]	
27.566703	tick[d]		
27.569405		rcv beat(0)[e]	
27.569481			rcv beat(1)
27.569533	rcv beat(0)		
27.569554	rcv beat(1)		
30.070266	tick[f]		
30.070464		rcv beat(0)	
30.070530			rcv beat(1)
30.070582	rcv beat(0)		
30.070603	rcv beat(1)		
40.070759	tick		
40.070970		rcv beat(0)	
40.071043			rcv beat(1)
40.071095	rcv beat(0)		
40.071116	rcv beat(1)[g]		

---

[a] p[1] is terminated.

[b] p[0] discovers that p[1] is not responding and reduces next period to 5 seconds.

[c] p[1] is restarted, but after the beat message is lost.

[d] p[0] discovers that p[1] did not respond to the last round and reduces the next period to 2.5 seconds.

[e] p[1] responds to the first beat message after restarting.

[f] p[0] discovers that p[1] is responding and sets next period to 10 seconds.

[g] The heartbeat has returned to normal.

Figure 7.14: Execution trace of accelerated heartbeat protocol with temporary failure of p[1].

	Log messages		
Seconds	$p[0]$	$p[1]$	$p[2]$
0.000000		start	
1.045771			start
3.033189	start		
3.033687		rcv beat(0)	
3.033777			rcv beat(1)
3.033841	rcv beat(0)		
3.033866	rcv beat(1)		
13.034061	tick		
13.034259		rcv beat(0)	
13.034329			rcv beat(1)
13.034382	rcv beat(0)		
13.034404	rcv beat(1)		
13.412154		terminate[a]	
23.034541	tick		
23.034775			rcv beat(1)
23.034838	rcv beat(1)		
33.035020	tick[b]		
33.035239			rcv beat(1)
33.035300	rcv beat(1)		
38.035266	tick		
38.035482			rcv beat(1)
38.035542	rcv beat(1)		
40.535881	tick		
40.536090			rcv beat(1)
40.536152	rcv beat(1)		
41.786962	tick		
41.787040	exit[c]		
69.536472			exit[d]

---

[a]$p[1]$ terminated.
[b]$p[0]$ discovers that $p[1]$ is not responding and reduces the next period.
[c]$p[0]$ terminated.
[d]$p[2]$ terminated.

Figure 7.15: Execution trace of accelerated heartbeat protocol with permanent failure of **p[1]**.

This page intentionally left blank

Chapter 8

A DNS SERVER

The Domain Name System[58, 59, 60], or DNS, is a distributed database mapping hierarchical keys, or *names,* to extensible, generalized values, or *resources.* The key features of the DNS are:

- The database is distributed among a large number of independently administered servers. This is a reliability and scaling feature as well as an administrative feature: the resources are replicated through several servers as well as being partitioned between groups of servers, avoiding any single point of failure for the DNS as a whole. Also, the administrative domain responsible for a given part of the data typically has authority over the servers for that part of the data.

- The key space is organized heirarchically, in a tree structure proceeding from an otherwise nameless root to top-level domains such as "edu," "com," and the two-letter ISO country code domains, and thence to second and lower-level domains such as "utexas" and "cs.utexas." This hierarchy roughly corresponds to the organizational and thus administrative structure of the data. Each name is made up of a sequence of labels and uniquely identifies a node in the hierarchy by beginning at the root and choosing a child node identified by the next label in the name.

- The values in the database are described by an extensible set of resource records, with each kind of resource record containing information useful for a different application. Each record is identified by a *class,* such as IN, the Internet class; and a *type* such as A, which provides an IPv4 address for the name of the node, or MX, which identifies the name and preference value for an Internet e-mail server for the name.

DNS is primarily described in RFC1034[58] and RFC1035[59] although extensions (particularly for security and internationalization) and new resource records are described in a large number of further RFCs. For this chapter, however, RFC 1034 and RFC 1035 are the only primary sources. In particular, DNSSEC[61] is not covered.

According to RFC 1034, the DNS consists of three components:

1. The tree-structured domain name space and the resource records for data associated with the names. The name space is administratively organized into *zones,* each consisting of a subtree of the name space. The root of each zone subtree is a node associated with a SOA (Start Of Authority) resource record and each zone contains the descendent nodes down to, but not including, any lower-level nodes with another SOA record. Since the descendent zones may be contained in a different DNS server, the parent zone needs to have enough information, called *glue,* for a client to contact the server for the child zone.

2. The name servers. A name server is a program holding information about the domain name space. Name servers perform two different, but related, roles:

   • An authoritative name server contains complete information about one or more zones, including all of the names in each zone, all of the records for those names, and the glue needed by sub-zones. Authoritative servers are divided into master servers and slave servers. A master server contains, by definition, up to date authoritative information about a zone. A slave server, on the other hand, contains authoritative information which may be out of date; slave servers get their information about zones by means of a *zone transfer* from the master server for the zone.

   • A caching name server contains incomplete information about any number of zones. For performance reasons, not every request for DNS information should result in a request to an authoritative server; since multiple requests are frequently made for the same information, requests from DNS clients may be satisfied from a local, caching server. To support caching, every record in a response from a DNS server contains a time-to-live, or TTL, field describing how long the record may be cached.

Some DNS server programs, such as the Berkeley Internet Name Domain, or BIND, are capable of performing both roles at the same time, but such usage is deprecated. Most other DNS server packages separate the two roles into two different programs and even BIND recommends that the two roles be separated into two hosts.

3. Resolvers. A resolver is a program which extracts information from the DNS for a client. A resolver is typically a library function such as gethostbyname called by a client program.

The DNS network protocol is very simple, normally consisting of a request and response. One complication is CNAME records, which provide aliases for domain names and which the server must follow in generating the response. Another complication is that a DNS query has four possible responses:

- An authoritative response that the given name does not exist.

- An authoritative response that, although the name exists, no record of the requested type for the given name exists.

- The resource record or records that were requested.

- A pointer to a sub-zone, indicating that, while the server is not capable of answering the query, a server for the indicated sub-zone may be able to.

The final possibility results in two possible further behaviors for the server:

- A server noting that it cannot answer a query may itself forward the query to a server for the sub-zone. This behavior is called a *recursive query,* and is the normal behavior for a caching server—it only responds to a client with the final answer, which is one of the first three possibilities.

- A server that cannot answer a query may respond with an indication that it cannot do so. This response will include the glue information needed by the requester to further track down the answer. This is the normal behavior of a non-caching, authoritative server.

The DNS network protocol for TCP/IP networks is capable of using two transport protocols, TCP or UDP. Typically, TCP is used only for large messages that will not fit into a single UDP datagram. These large messages are usually zone transfers; almost all other DNS requests and responses use UDP.

While performance is not a key requirement for the DNS system, it is a very important attribute for a DNS server, since the DNS is an important part of the Internet infrastructure, the databases needed for some zones are very large, and many servers must respond to a large volume of requests.[62,63, 64, 65]

The remainder of this chapter presents an implementation of an authoritative DNS server process, called aserv, based around a protocol specification given in TAP. The specifications and code for this implementation is available as part of the *apdns* package from the Austin Protocol Compiler home page.

The authoritative DNS server

```
message query
begin
    id : 16 bits,
    type : 1 bit = 0,
    opcode : 4 bits,
    aa : 1 bit,
    tc : 1 bit,
    rd : 1 bit,
    ra : 1 bit,
    z : 3 bits,
    rcode : 4 bits,
    qdcount : 16 bits,
    ancount : 16 bits,
    nscount : 16 bits,
    arcount : 16 bits,
    body : size - 12 bytes
end
```

Figure 8.1: A DNS query message. The DNS response message, named "resp" in the TAP definition, is the same except that the type field is a constant 1.

The TAP definition of a DNS query message is shown in Figure 8.1. The format of a response message is the same, except the type field is set to 1. These messages consist of two parts: a header and a body. In the TAP definition, all but the last field make up the header part. Header fields are used as follows:

- The id field is a unique number identifying the request.

- The opcode field indicates the type of the query, normally a standard query. Other options include an inverse query and a server status request, neither of which are addressed here.

- The aa field is used in a response message, indicating that the server responding is authoritative for the name in the query.

- The tc field is used in a response messages to indicate that the response is too large to fit in the message and has been truncated.

- The rd field is set in the query message when the requester wants the server to pursue the query recursively; a normal client might set this while a caching server making a query might not.

- The ra field is used in a response message to indicate whether or not the server is willing to recursively pursue queries; an authoritative server may not be.

- The z field is reserved for future use and should be set to 0.

- The rcode field is used in a response message to indicate the results of the query as follows:

  0 No error condition.

  1 The name server was unable to interpret the query.

  2 The name server was unable to process this query due to a problem with the name server.

  3 The domain name referenced in the query does not exist.

  4 The name server does not support the requested kind of query.

  5 The name server refuses to perform the specified operation for policy reasons.

The remaining fields refer to sections in the message body and are discussed later.

The body part of a DNS message, either a query or a response, is made up of four sections:

- A query section containing the request being made. The query consists of a name, a type and a class. The number of entries in the query section is given by the qdcount field in the header; it is normally one. For query messages, the remaining sections of the body are empty. For response messages, the query section is copied over and the remaining sections contain the response information.

- An answer section containing the resource records answering the query. The ancount field of the header gives the number of records in the answer section.

- An authority section containing NS (name server) resource records. Some servers add these records to describe the authority for any answer, which aids caching for future requests. However, the contents of this section are only needed when the server is not capable of answering the query and is not willing to pursue it recursively. The NS records are part of the glue telling the requester where to go next. The nscount field gives the number of records in this section.

- An additional information section. When the responding server cannot answer the query and is returning glue information, it normally puts address records into the additional information section. These address records match the NS records in the authority section, and are also part of the glue information telling the requester where to go next. The arcount field gives the number of records in this section.

Common parts of the body sections of a DNS message are names. Since DNS messages may contain many names or many copies of the same name (as part of multiple resource records, for example), the names use a compression scheme. Each name is made up of one or more labels, and in a message each label is represented by a length byte followed by the corresponding number of bytes making up the label. However, since each label is limited to 64 bytes, the two high bits of the length must be zero. The compression scheme uses these two bits differently: if instead the two high bits are one, the remaining six bits of the length byte plus the next byte are taken as an offset in the message. The label found at that offset, plus any following labels, are used as the remainder of the current name.

Because the sizes and formats of the four body sections are variable, they cannot be described in TAP. Instead, the body of the message must be parsed by external C code during the processing of the message, as seen in Figure 8.3.

```
process aserv
var c : address;
    fnd, invld : integer
begin
  rcv query from c →
    resp.id, resp.opcode, resp.rd := query.id, query.opcode, query.rd;
    resp.ra, resp.aa := 0, 1;
    resp.qdcount := query.qdcount;
    invld := parse_query(query.qdcount, query.body);
    if invld → resp.rcode := response_code();           /* rcode = error code */
             resp.ancount, resp.nscount, resp.arcount :=
               query.ancount, query.nscount, query.arcount;
             resp.tc, resp.body, resp.size :=
               query.tc, query.body, query.size
    | ¬invld → ...                                       /* See Figure 8.3. */
             resp.tc := response_oversize();
             resp.body, resp.size := response_body(), response_size() + 12
    fi;
    send resp to c
end
```

Figure 8.2: The authoritative DNS server process, part 1.

Figure 8.2 and Figure 8.3 present the authoritative DNS server process, aserv. This process has a single action, which receives a DNS query message. Upon receiving the query, the action begins building a response by copying fields from the query and setting the recursion available flag to zero and the authoritative answer flag to one. Then it calls the C function parse_query. The parse_query function checks the query for unsupported options such as a

```
fnd := query_database();
resp.rcode := response_code();                    /* either NXDOMAIN or NOERROR */
if fnd = 0 →                                       /* name and record found */
    resp.ancount, resp.nscount, resp.arcount :=
      response_ancount(), response_nscount(), response_arcount()
|  fnd = 1 →                                       /* response points to subdomain */
   resp.aa, resp.ancount, resp.nscount, resp.arcount :=
      0, response_ancount(), response_nscount(), response_arcount()
|  fnd = 2 →                                       /* rcode = NXDOMAIN: no name */
   resp.ancount, resp.nscount, resp.arcount := 0, 0, 0
|  fnd = 3 →                                       /* rcode = NOERROR: no record */
   resp.ancount, resp.nscount, resp.arcount := 0, 0, 0
fi;
```

Figure 8.3: The authoritative DNS server process, part 2.

zone transfer request or multiple query records in the query section, converts the query to an internal form, and begins to prepare a response message by storing the query record in the query section of the response buffer. Finally, parse_query returns a flag indicating whether the query message is valid or not.

If the query is invalid, the response's rcode field is set appropriately and the remainder of the response is copied from the query message.

If the query is valid, the action in aserv calls the C function query_database, attempts to locate one or more records satisfying the query. Figure 8.4 presents the algorithm used by the query_database function. The return value of the query_database function determines the contents of the response message:

- If query_response returns 0, records matching the query have been found and must be copied into the response buffer, as well as setting the remaining fields of the header such as ancount.

- If query_response returns 1, records representing glue information must be copied into the response buffer. In this case, however, the response is not authoritative.

- If query_response returns 2 or 3, no further records need to be copied since the rcode field contains the distinguishing information.

The buffer containing the stored records for the response is returned by the response_body function.

1. Locate resources records matching the name from the query.

2. If matching records are found,

> *(a) Select records matching the type and class of the query.*
>
> *(b) If such records are found, save them to be stored in the response. In this case, query_database returns 0.*
>
> *(c) If no such records are found, nothing will be stored in the response and query_database returns 1.*
>
> *In either case, the rcode field of the response will indicate success.*

3. If no records matching the name from the query are found,

> *(a) Attempt to locate nameserver records for a sub-zone containing the name from the query.*
>
> *(b) If no suitable NS records are found, nothing will be stored in the response and query_database returns 2. The rcode field of the response will be set to NXDO-MAIN, indicating no name exists.*
>
> *(c) If an NS record is found, store it and the related glue information for use in the response. In this case, query_database returns 3. The rcode field of the response will indicate success.*

Figure 8.4: Algorithm for query_database.

Behind the parse_query and query_database functions lie almost all of the complexity of the DNS server. This complexity comes from the difficulty in parsing the query body, supporting the database, and generating the response body. When managing this complexity, a key advantage of the Austin Protocol Compiler design becomes vital: Since the compiler generates C code, any tools available to C programs are also available when implementing protocols. In this case, the DNS server implementation uses the Flex and Bison parser generator tools and the Boehm-Demers-Weiser conservative garbage collector[66,67]. Flex and Bison are used to parse the DNS database information, from the RFC1035-formatted master files. The garbage collector provides memory management for the database and for DNS message handling.

The current implementation described here has a number of limitations. In addition to not dealing with extensions to the basic DNS protocol, it also uses a very simplistic database which limits the contents of the database to a single zone, along with the glue needed for sub-zones. The database is also inefficient for large domains. Also, no guarantees are made about the correctness of the implementation—the specification is complex and not always clear and this implementation has undergone only minimal interoperability testing.

Implementation performance

As mentioned previously, the performance of a DNS server is important. In order to analyze the performance of protocols implemented with the Austin Protocol Compiler, we compared the implementation of the DNS server described in this chapter with two other commonly used server implementations.

The Berkeley Internet Name Domain[68], or BIND, software is de facto standard DNS software implementation. It includes a name resolver library and tools for querying and administering the DNS as well as a DNS server. The BIND DNS server, named, is capable of acting as both an authoritative server and a caching server although the Internet Systems Consortium, the producers of BIND, recommend administratively separating the two functions. The named server also implements essentially every option for the DNS protocols, including supporting TCP connections, zone transfers, and the DNSSEC security extensions. Finally, the database of DNS information stored by the named server is kept in the server's memory.

D. J. Bernstein produces djbdns[69], another DNS software implementation. In contrast to BIND, djbdns divides server functionality between a number of programs, including an authoritative name server, tinydns, and a caching name server, dnscache. An additional program, axfrdns, supports TCP connections for zone transfers; tinydns, for example, only supports UDP queries. The primary requirements for the djbdns software are correctness and security; one result is that the database of DNS information is stored in the server's filesystem.

The server described in this chapter, aserv, shares some features with both named and tinydns. Like named, it reads zone information from an RFC 1035-formatted master file and keeps the database in memory; djbdns supplies another program which parses zone information from a configuration file in a non-RFC1035 format and writes it to a binary database file used by tinydns. On the other hand, aserv is designed to behave more like tinydns in not handling zone transfers or a caching service.

We used BIND version 9.2.3, apdns version 0.9, and djbdns version 1.05 in these measurements. The client programs for each test are part of the apdns package and use the Poslib[70] DNS library version 1.0.2. The default optimization and code generation configurations were used for all packages.[1]

The server host is an AMD Athlon XP 2200+ running at 1800MHz with 512MB of memory, using Linux kernel version 2.6.0. The client host for the remote measurements is a 1333MHz Intel Celeron with 256MB of memory, using Linux kernel version 2.4.18. Both machines were in single user mode during the measurements, with only required system processes running. The two machines are connected via a 100Mb/s ethernet, with a measured throughput (via nttcp[71]) of 7.2MB/S.

Since the quality of the database is not relevant to the protocol implementation, a small database containing only a few records was created for each server. The master file used by BIND's named and apdns's aserv is shown in Figure 8.5; an equivalent configuration was created for djbdns's tinydns.

There are three components to a network protocol implementation's temporal performance:

1. Latency, or the time a single request or transfer takes,

2. Throughput, or the number of requests (or the amount of data transferred) that the implementation can handle in a unit time period, and

3. Overhead, or the processing time per request that the implementation takes outside of that to directly satisfy the request.

---

[1]It is interesting to note that these measurements provide an extreme example of the compatibility problems of network protocol development. The comparison is between three unrelated implementations of the authoritative server process of the DNS protocol, made using an implementation of the client process that is itself unrelated to any of the servers. One of the servers, named, implements essentially every enhancement and extension made since the original development of the DNS protocol; another, tinydns, only implements a chosen, production-quality subset of them; and the third, aserv, does not implement any and is not complete with regard to the features of the original DNS specification. Yet in the end, all must work compatibly to make the measurements.

```
example.com. IN 86400 SOA a.example.com. hostmaster.example.com. (
              2 ; Serial
              10800 ; Refresh: 3 hours
              3600 ; Retry: 1 hour
              86400 ; Expire: 1 day
              3600 ; Negative caching TTL: 1 hour)
example.com. IN 86400 NS a.example.com.
a.example.com. IN 86400 A 172.16.0.1
1.0.16.172.in-addr.arpa. IN 86400 PTR a.example.com.
b.example.com. IN 86400 A 172.16.0.2
2.0.16.172.in-addr.arpa. IN 86400 PTR b.example.com.
below.example.com. IN 1024 NS c.below.example.com.
c.below.example.com. IN 1024 A 172.16.0.3
```

Figure 8.5: Master file used by the BIND and apdns servers.

These three components are clearly related; latency and throughput are approximately inverses. The overhead, however, alters that basic relationship. For example, it is possible to optimize for reduced latency by moving computations that are needed by the protocol but unnecessary to a current request outside of a "critical path" for the request. The result is an implementation with improved latency but unchanged throughput (or perhaps worse throughput, if shifting the overhead computation has costs). In any case, the three components are separately important, since a protocol implementation should be capable of responding to a request quickly, be capable of responding to a large number of requests, and avoid consuming resources needed elsewhere by the server.

Latency

The latency and throughput measurements were taken in two configurations:

- A remote configuration with the DNS client processes executing on a client host and the server executing on a server host and

- A local configuration with the client and the server both executing on the server host.

Miss rate		Remote aserv	named	tinydns
0%	mean	354	398	399
	std. dev.	74.4	47.9	45.4
25%	mean	341	407	391
	std. dev.	75.6	53.8	46.0
50%	mean	341	402	394
	std. dev.	72.7	45.2	64.2
Miss rate		Local aserv	named	tinydns
0%	mean	98	187	109
	std. dev.	73.9	14.7	8.3
25%	mean	97	192	111
	std. dev.	69.9	12.6	9.2
50%	mean	92	188	108
	std. dev.	64.9	14.7	11.6

Latency (μsec)

Figure 8.6: DNS server request latency. A lower value is better.

The first configuration gives a view of the performance in a network setting while the second removes the costs of network communication, which have a tendency to conceal the differences between the systems.

The latency of DNS queries is measured by recording the start time, making a query, waiting for a response, and reporting the length of the interval between the start time and the completion time. The program which performed this measurement reads 100,000 queries from a file sequentially. Three input files were generated for the measurements:

1. A list containing only queries in the database; all of the queries matched records in the server's database.

2. A list with a 25% miss rate: 25% of the queries are not in the database, with an even mix of missing domain names and missing records.

3. A list with a 50% miss rate.

Figure 8.6 shows the results of the latency measurements, including the mean latency for the 100,000 queries and the standard deviation of the latencies. Two features are clear: the aserv server has less consistency in its latency, leading to the larger standard deviations, and the aserv has a lower latency, although not significantly lower than tinydns.

The differences in latency are not necessarily meaningful; the aserv server has less functionality than tinydns and much less than named, so the comparison is not wholly valid. However, the performance of the Austin Protocol Compiler-generated server is not completely out of reach.

Throughput

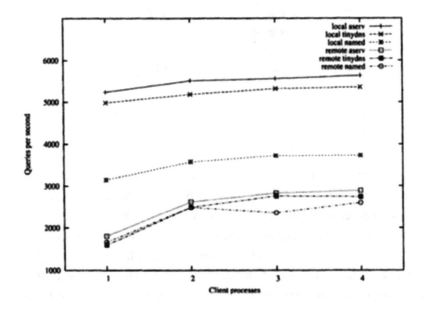

Figure 8.7: DNS server request throughput. A higher value is better.

The basic throughput measurements use a program which make 100,000 queries and reports the length of the interval between starting the queries and completing them. Since there was only a minimal difference between the three different database miss rates in the latency measurement, only the 0% miss rate file was used for the throughput and overhead measurements.

Since each query requires a certain amount of turn-around time, while the client is parsing the previous response and preparing the next query, the basic throughput measurement does not adequately show the server throughput. To close in on the potential throughput, several client processes were executed simultaneously, making requests from the same server. The potential throughput is conceptually the asymptote of the curve described by the throughput of the server as the number of client processes increases.

Figure 8.7 shows these curves, for both configurations of each of the three servers. The remote configurations cluster at the bottom of the graph—this shows the effects of the network communication costs in concealing the difference between the servers. In both configurations, however, the BIND named server has the lowest throughput; presumably because it is the largest, most complex of the programs. The tinydns server and the aserv server are again fairly close together, with a perhaps meaningless advantage to aserv.

Overhead

	CPU time (sec)		
	User time	System time	Total
named	3.44	3.22	6.66
tinydns	1.52	3.43	4.95
aserv	1.19	2.09	3.28

Figure 8.8: DNS server CPU overhead. A lower value is better.

The final measurement is the overhead of the server, taken while the server responds to 100,000 queries from the latency client in the remote configuration. The measurements were taken using the program *time,* a tool to summarize system resources usage. The two portions of the CPU overhead are user time, showing the CPU time spent by the process itself, and system time, showing CPU time spent by the operating system kernel on behalf of the process— performing I/O, for example.

Again in this figure, aserv shows the lowest total cost as well as the lowest independent system and user times. Again, this is presumably because named is a large, complex program, while tinydns takes the approach of opening, accessing, and closing its database file on each query—hence the larger system time for it.

Performance of the Austin Protocol Compiler

The measurements in this chapter are not meant to attempt to show that apdns's aserv is in any way better than either named or tinydns. The aserv implementation is deficient in many ways. However, the measurements do demonstrate that the performance of an Austin Protocol Compiler-based system is entirely reasonable.

Performance, measured as either throughput, latency, or overhead, has not been a major driver for the design of the Austin Protocol Compiler. So far, though, the performance of the simple implementation has been entirely adequate. If performance does become a limiting factor, the design of the Austin Protocol Compiler has some openings for possible performance improvement.

- In the current system, message recognition is integrated with message parsing. The recognition/parsing process is attempted for each receive action without favoring any action. However, it should be clear from the discussion of the message handling functions on page 74 that message recognition in the Austin Protocol Compiler is easily translatable to a packet filter approach[72]. With a packet filter system built into the protocol engine, the runtime system could directly dispatch the appropriate receive action.

- In a similar situation, the current system does not favor any action when attempting to execute the local actions. An approach to limiting the search for enabled local actions would be to have the compiler identify two sets of variables for each action:

  1. The set of variables used in the guard of the action. This set will be empty for receive and timeout actions, but will be non-empty for reasonable local actions. This set is called the *guard set*.

  2. The set of variables possibly modified by statements of the action. This set is called the *watched set*.

Using the guard and modified sets, it is possible to deduce the chaining behavior of the process's actions by finding the set of local actions which may have been enabled by the execution of another the of actions.

Beginning in a state where all of the local actions are disabled, the only possible step in the process is the receipt of a message or the expiration of a timeout delay. Following one of those events, the runtime system can maintain a set of possibly enabled local actions, called *trial actions,* built from the watched set of the action handling the event and the guard sets of the local actions. The trial actions would then be attempted in turn. When a local action is attempted and found to be enabled, the other local actions which may be chained from it are also added to the trial actions. (An executed action must also be re-added to the set, since it may not have disabled itself.) Actions are removed from the trial set when they are attempted and found to be disabled. Although there are degenerate cases, when implementing a reasonable protocol this scheme should result in fewer attempted actions. For example, it correctly covers the cases of the two examples from Chapter 7, where the initial action is executed once and need never be examined again.

Both of these enhancements would introduce considerable complexity into the Austin Protocol Compiler. So far, neither seems worthwhile, since they address scaling issues in the protocol specification (the first for larger numbers of receivable messages and the second for larger numbers of local actions).

This page intentionally left blank

Chapter 9

CONCLUDING REMARKS

Summary

In Chapter 1, we identified three classes of problems that, in combination, uniquely apply to network protocol development:

1. Intrinsic problems, made up of the problems of safety and liveness, errors and security associated with any distributed or parallel program.

2. Extrinsic problems, made up of the problems presented by the environment of the network protocol, and

3. Compatibility problems, made up of the difficulties of protocol interoperability, protocol extensions, and future protocol enhancements.

   In the intervening chapters, we presented the Timed Abstract Protocol notation, a small, formal language intended for describing asynchronous, message passing network protocols. We also presented two execution models for TAP: an abstract execution model suited for protocol design, comprehension, and verification, and a concrete execution model suited for easy implementation. We then argued that the two models are equivalent: that a protocol under the concrete model preserves the intended behavior of the protocol given under the abstract model.

The equivalence between the abstract execution model and the concrete execution model yields two further points:

- The practice of using high-level abstractions to specify and verify network protocols is entirely valid, as long as the abstractions can be preserved by lower-level constructs.

- The practice of using low-level constructs to implement network protocols is also valid, as long as these constructs preserve the abstract behavior of the protocl.

We also described the Austin Protocol Compiler, a system that transforms a TAP specification of a protocol process into executable C code and that provides an runtime environment for that code. We finally showed several examples of protocols implemented using APC.

The final question is how the Timed Abstract Protocol notation and Austin Protocol Compiler satisfy the three classes of problems from the first chapter.

- TAP, under the abstract model, is a powerful tool for describing, comprehension, and verifying network protocols. As such, it is well suited for handling the intrinsic problems, since such problems exist within the protocol itself and are capable of being formally described.

- APC, in combination with TAP, is a powerful tool for implementing network protocols. By allowing a protocol to be written, modified, and made executable quickly and easily, TAP and APC allow extrinsic problems to be identified experimentally and allow various approaches for handling them to be explored.

- TAP combined with APC is a powerful tool for specifying network protocols. By allowing the protocol to be understood in isolation from the application around it and by easily providing a reference implementation, the combination eases interoperability problems. Also, since the combination exposes the protocol as a separate entity, it better shows openings for protocol extensions and enhancements.

Future directions

The development of the Timed Abstract Protocol notation and the Austin Protocol Compiler, as described here, is fundamentally complete. However, a number of interesting questions remain open and a number of research avenues are unexplored.

Enhancements

The Timed Abstract Protocol notation, along with the abstract and concrete execution models, is quite effective at describing asynchronous, message passing network protocols. The limitations placed on the execution models, in particular, support the development of most network protocols by limiting the potential effects of faults to the most common problems.

However, a worthwhile direction for research is to investigate changes to the language and to the abstract and concrete execution models to handle events such as process failures and security violations.

What is needed is a precise definition of the effects of each additional feature, in both execution models, and an investigation of the changes to the models and the equivalence relationship needed to accommodate the feature.

Alternative compiler back ends

The Austin Protocol Compiler implementation currently produces portable C. While it would be fairly trivial to create other modules to produce code in different programming languages, more interesting alternatives involve generating code or specifications for special purposes:

- A model checker such as SPIN[37, 38], **Murɸ[28]**, or TLC[34]. While TAP provides strong assumptions in order to ease verification and finite-state model checking has serious limits, model checkers have proved useful[29]. An alternative back end that produces input for a model checker would easily provide mechanical validation of some protocols.

  Such a back end would also require changes to TAP, which currently has no way of specifying the properties that the model checker should validate.

- A network simulator such as ns2[73]. Some properties of network protocols, such as congestion behavior and interaction with other protocols, are not easily amenable to verification. Frequently, these network protocols are also difficult or expensive to implement. In these instances, a network simulator provides feedback to the protocol designer and concrete information to potential protocol implementors.

Alternative runtime systems

Currently, the only available basis network protocol is UDP. However, the implementation separates the runtime library into the generic runtime engine and support functions, and the basis network protocol interface. Providing additional basis network protocols, such as IP or any other asynchronous message-passing protocol, would be a simple extension. The only major requirement is that the protocol be supported by the BSD socket interface and this requirement could be removed with some work.

It would also be possible, although not necessarily as simple, to use a non-message-passing protocol, such as the stream-oriented TCP, as a base protocol. While we have not investigated the necessary changes, it is clear that the message recognition approach would need to be modified since TCP does not preserve message boundaries.

A third exciting possibility would be the use of APC in entirely different environments, such as resource-constrained embedded systems like networked sensors[74]. The constraints on these systems, both in terms of computation and in terms of the network architecture created when the sensors are deployed put most common network protocols out of reach. Yet the same constraints require more out from the network protocol used among the sensors and between the sensors and a base station.

BIBLIOGRAPHY

[1] Tim Berners-Lee, Roy T. Fielding, and Henrik Frystyk Nielsen. Hypertext transfer protocol – HTTP/1.0. Internet Engineering Task Force RFC1945, May 1996.

[2] W. Richard Stevens. *TCP/IP Illustrated: The Protocols,* volume 1. Addison Wesley, 1994.

[3] W. Richard Stevens. *TCP/IP Illustrated: TCP for Transactions, HTTP, NNTP, and the UNIX Domain Protocols,* volume 3. Addison Wesley, 1996.

[4] Simon E. Spero. Analysis of HTTP performance problems. http://www.ibiblio.org/mdma-release/http-prob.html, January 2004.

[5] Hari Balakrishnan, Venkata N. Padmanabhan, Srinivasan Seshan, Mark Stemm, and Randy H. Katz. TCP behavior of a busy internet server: Analysis and improvements. In *INFOCOM (1),* March 1998.

[6] R. Fielding, J. Gettys, J. Mogul, H. Frystyk, L. Masinter, P. Leach, and T. Berners-Lee. Hypertext transfer protocol – HTTP/1.1. Internet Engineering Task Force RFC2616, June 1999.

[7] Scott Bradner. The internet standards process — revision 3. Internet Engineering Task Force RFC2026, October 1996.

[8] Gary R. Wright and W. Richard Stevens. *TCP/IP Illustrated: The Implementation,* volume 2. Addison Wesley, 1995.

[9] John Nagle. Congestion control in IP/TCP internetworks. Internet Engineering Task Force RFC896, January 1984.

[10] Greg Minshall, Yasushi Saito, Jeffrey C. Mogul, and Ben Verghese. Application performance pitfalls and TCP's Nagle algorithm. In *Workshop on Internet Server Performance,* May 1999.

[11] M. A. Padlipsky. *The Elements of Networking Style.* iUniverse.com, 2000. Originally published by Prentice-Hall, 1985.

[12] Norman C. Hutchinson and Larry L. Peterson. The x-Kernel: An architecture for implementing network protocols. *IEEE Transactions on Software Engineering,* 17(1), January 1991.

[13] Larry L. Peterson and Bruce S. Davie. *Computer Networks: A Systems Approach.* Morgan Kaufmann, first edition, 1996. (The second edition removes references to the x-Kernel.).

[14] J. Mogul and S. Deering. Path MTU discovery. Internet Engineering Task Force RFC1191, November 1990.

[15] K. K. Ramakrishnan, Sally Floyd, and David L. Black. The addition of explicit congestion notification (ECN) to IP. Internet Engineering Task Force RFC3168, September 2001.

[16] Bob Braden, Ted Faber, and Mark Handley. From protocol stack to protocol heap –
      role-based architecture (RBA). Presentation, ACM HotNets I, October 2002.
      http://www.isi.edu/newarch/.

[17] Robert Braden, Ted Faber, and Mark Handley. From protocol stack to protocol
      heap—role-based architecture. In *First Workshop on Hot Topics in Networks,* October
      2002.

[18] Ken Birman, Robert Constable, Mark Hayden, Christopher Kreitz, Ohad Rodeh, Robbert
      van Renesse, and Werner Vogels. The Horus and Ensemble projects: Accomplishments
      and limitations. In *Proceedings of the DARPA Information Survivability Conference &
      Exposition (DISCEX '00),* January 2000.

[19] Mark G. Hayden. *The Ensemble System.* PhD thesis, Cornell University, January 1998.

[20] Marshall T. Rose. *BEEP: The Definitive Guide.* O'Reilly and Associates, March 2002.

[21] Marshall T. Rose. The blocks extensible exchange protocol core. Internet Engineering
      Task Force RFC3080, March 2001.

[22] Marshall T. Rose. On the design of application protocols. Internet Engineering Task
      Force RFC3117, November 2001.

[23] Eddie Kohler. Prolac, a language for protocol compilation. Master's thesis,
      Massachusetts Institute of Technology, 1997.

[24] Eddie Kohler, M. Frans Kaashoek, and David R. Montgomery. A readable TCP in the
      Prolac protocol language. In *SIGCOMM,* 1999.

[25] Mark B. Abbot and Larry L. Peterson. A language-based approach to protocol
      implementation. *IEEE/ACM Transactions on Networking,* 1(1), September 1993.

[26] A. Basu, G. Morrisett, and T. von Eicken. Promela++: A language for constructing
      correct and efficient protocols. In *Proceedings of the Conference on Computer
      Communications (IEEE Infocom),* San Francisco, CA, March/April 1998.

[27] Satish Chandra, Brad Richards, and James R. Larus. Teapot: Language support for
      writing memory coherence protocols. In *Proceedings of the SIGPLAN conference on
      Programming Language Design and Implementation (PLDI),* May 1996. Also appears in
      ACM SIGPLAN Notices, 31(5), 1996.

[28] David L. Dill, Andreas J. Drexler, Alan J. Hu, and C. Han Yang. Protocol verification as a
      hardware design aid. In *International Conference on Computer Design,* 1992.

[29] S. Chandra, J. R. Larus, M. Dahlin, B. Richards, R. Y. Wang, and T. E. Anderson.
      Experience with a language for writing coherence protocols. In *Proc. of the USENIX
      Conference on Domain-Specific Languages (DSL),* 1997.

[30] Sanjeev Kumar, Yitzhak Mandelbaum, Xiang Yu, and Kai Li. ESP: A language for
      programmable devices. In *Proceedings of ACM Conference on Programming Language
      Design and Implementation (PLDI),* June 2001.

[31] Sanjeev Kumar and Kai Li. Performance impact of using ESP to implement VMMC
      firmware. In *Proceedings of ACM Workshop on Novel Uses of System Area Networks
      (SAN),* January 2002.

[32] Sanjeev Kumar and Kai Li. Using model checking to debug device firmware. In
      *Proceedings of USENIX Symposium on Operating Systems Design and Implementation
      (OSDI),* December 2002.

[33] K. Mani Chandy and Jayadev Misra. *Parallel Program Design: A Foundation.* Addison-Wesley, May 1989.

[34] Leslie Lamport. *Specifying Systems: The TLA+ Language and Tools for Hardware and Software Engineers.* Addison-Wesley, 2002.

[35] Kenneth J. Turner. *Using Formal Description Techniques: An Introduction to Estelle, LOTOS, and SDL.* John Wiley & Sons, 1993.

[36] Andrei Serjantov, Peter Sewell, and Keith Wansbrough. The UDP calculus: Rigorous semantics for real networking. In *Theoretical Aspects of Computer Software (TACS),* October 2001. Also in Lecture Notes in Computer Science 2215.

[37] Gerard J. Holzmann. *Design and Validation of Computer Protocols.* Prentice Hall, 1991.

[38] Gerard J. Holzmann. The model checker SPIN. *IEEE Transactions on Software Engineering,* 23(5), May 1997.

[39] Gerard J. Holzmann. *The SPIN Model Checker: Primer and Reference Manual.* Addison-Wesley, 2004.

[40] Gérard Berry. The foundations of Esterel. In G. Plotkin, C. Stirling, and M. Tofte, editors, *Proof, Language and Interaction: Essays in Honour of Robin Milner.* MIT Press, 1998.

[41] Claude Castelluccia, Walid Dabbous, and Sean O'Malley. Generating efficient protocol code from an abstract specification. *IEEE/ACM Transactions on Networking,* 5(4), 1997.

[42] Mohamed G. Gouda. *Elements of Network Protocol Design.* John Wiley and Sons, 1998.

[43] J. Postel. Transmission control protocol. Internet Engineering Task Force RFC793, September 1981.

[44] R. T. Braden. Requirements for internet hosts—communication layers. Internet Engineering Task Force RFC1122, October 1989.

[45] Olivier Dubuisson. *ASN.1: Communication Between Heterogeneous Systems.* Morgan Kaufmann, 2001. Translated by Philippe Fouquart.

[46] R. Srinivasan. XDR: External data representation standard. Internet Engineering Task Force RFC 1832, August 1995.

[47] Paolo A. G. Sivilotti. A class of synchronization systems that permit the use of large atomic blocks. In *Proceedings of CASCON '98,* December 1998.

[48] Richard J. Lipton. Reduction: A method of proving properties of parallel programs. *Communications of the ACM,* 6(2), April 1975. Described in [49].

[49] Leslie Lamport and Fred B. Schneider. Pretending atomicity. Technical Report 44, Digital Systems Research Center, May 1989.

[50] Leslie Lamport. A theorem on atomicity in distributed systems. *Distributed Computing,* 4(2), 1990.

[51] CERT advisory CA-1998-01: Smurf IP denial-of-service attacks, January 1998. http://www.cert.org/advisories/CA-1998-01 .html.

[52] J. Postel. Internet control message protocol. Internet Engineering Task Force RFC792, September 1981.

[53] CERT advisory CA-1996-21: TCP SYN flooding and IP spoofing attacks, September 1996. http://www.cert.org/advisories/CA-1996-21.html.

[54] M.G. Gouda, E.N. Elnozahy, C.-T. Huang, and T.M. McGuire. Hop integrity in computer networks. *IEEE/ACM Transactions on Networking,* 10(3), June 2002.

[55] Paul Ferguson and Daniel Senie. Network ingress filtering: Defeating denial of service attacks which employ ip source address spoofing. Internet Engineering Task Force RFC2827, May 2000.

[56] M.G. Gouda and Tommy M. McGuire. Accelerated heartbeat protocols. In *Proceedings of the 18th International Conference on Distributed Computing Systems,* May 1998.

[57] M.G. Gouda and Tommy M. McGuire. Alert communication primitives in TCP. *Journal of High Speed Networks,* 9(2), 2000.

[58] P. Mockapetris. Domain names - concepts and facilities. Internet Engineering Task Force RFC1034, November 1987.

[59] P. Mockapetris. Domain names - implementation and specification. Internet Engineering Task Force RFC1035, November 1987.

[60] Paul Albitz and Cricket Liu. *DNS and BIND.* O'Reilly and Associates, fourth edition, 2001.

[61] D. Eastlake. Domain name system security extensions. Internet Engineering Task Force RFC2535, March 1999.

[62] Peter B. Danzig, Katia Obraczka, and Anant Kumar. An analysis of wide-area name server traffic: A study of the internet domain name system. In *Proceedings of ACM SIGCOMM,* January 1992.

[63] Christian Huitema and Sam Weerahandi. Internet measurements: the rising tide and the DNS snag. In *ITC Specialist Seminar, IP Traffic Measurement, Modeling and Management,* September 2000.

[64] Richard Liston, Sridhar Srinivasan, and Ellen Zegura. Diversity in DNS performance measures. In *2nd Internet Measurement Workshop,* November 2002.

[65] Jaeyeon Jung, Emil Sit, Hari Balakrishnan, and Robert Morris. DNS performance and the effectiveness of caching. In *IEEE/ACM Trans. on Networking,* October 2002.

[66] H. Boehm and M. Weiser. Garbage collection in an uncooperative environment. *Software Practice and Experience,* September 1988.

[67] Hans Boehm. A garbage collector for C and C++. http://www.hpl.hp.com/personal/Hans_Boehm/gc/, March 2004.

[68] Internet Systems Consortium, Inc. ISC BIND. http://www.isc.org/index.pl?/sw/bind/, March 2004.

[69] D. J. Bernstein, djbdns. http://cr.yp.to/djbdns.html, March 2004.

[70] Meilof Veeningen. Poslib DNS library. http://posadis.sourceforge.net/projects/poslib.php, March 2004.

[71] Elmar Bartel. New TTCP program. http://www.leo.org/~elmar/nttcp/, March 2004.

[72] Masanobu Yuhara, Brian N. Bershad, Chris Maeda, and J. Eliot B. Moss. Efficient packet demultiplexing for multiple endpoints and large messages. In *USENIX Winter,* 1994.

[73] The VINT Project. *The ns Manual,* April 2002. http://www.isi.edu/nsnam/ns/ns-documentation.html.

[74] Jason Hill, Robert Szewczyk, Alec Woo, Seth Hollar, David Culler, and Kristofer Pister. System architecture directions for network sensors. In *ASPLOS 2000,* November 2000.

INDEX